WITH RENEWED STRENGTH

JOURNEYS OF EAGLES *who* SOAR

VOLUME II

20TH YEAR ANNIVERSARY EDITION

AN ANTHOLOGY PROJECT

Copyright © 2025 Eagles International Training Institute

Scripture quotations marked KJV are from the King James Version and are in the public domain. Scripture quotations marked NKJV are taken from the New King James Version®, Copyright © 1982 by Thomas Nelson, and used by permission. All rights reserved. Scripture quotations marked NIV are taken from the Holy Bible, New International Version®, NIV®, Copyright © 1973, 1978, 1984, 2011 by Biblica, Inc.™ Used by permission. All rights reserved worldwide. Scripture quotations marked NASB are taken from the New American Standard Bible®, Copyright © 1960, 1962, 1963, 1968, 1971, 1972, 1973, 1975, 1977, 1995, 2020 by The Lockman Foundation. Used by permission. All rights reserved. (www.lockman.org). Scripture quotations marked NLT are taken from the Holy Bible, New Living Translation, Copyright © 1996, 2004, 2015 by Tyndale House Foundation. Used by permission of Tyndale House Publishers, Inc., Carol Stream, Illinois 60188. All rights reserved. Scripture quotations marked AMP are taken from the Amplified Bible, Copyright © 1954, 1958, 1962, 1964, 1965, 1987 by The Lockman Foundation, La Habra, California 90631. All rights reserved. Scripture quotations marked ESV are from The Holy Bible, English Standard Version®, ESV® Text Edition: 2016, Copyright © 2001 by Crossway, a publishing ministry of Good News Publishers. Used by permission. All rights reserved. Scripture quotations marked MSG are taken from The Message, Copyright © 1993, 1994, 1995, 1996, 2000, 2001, 2002 by Eugene H. Peterson. Used by permission of NavPress. All rights reserved. Scripture quotations marked TPT are from The Passion Translation®, TPT®, Copyright © 2017, 2018, 2020 by Passion & Fire Ministries, Inc. Used by permission. All rights reserved. Scripture quotations marked TLB are taken from The Living Bible, Copyright © 1971 by Tyndale House Foundation. Used by permission of Tyndale House Publishers, Inc., Carol Stream, Illinois 60188. All rights reserved. Scripture quotations marked CJSB are from The Complete Jewish Study Bible, Copyright © 2016 by Hendrickson Publishers, Peabody, MA. All rights reserved. No part of this document may be reproduced or transmitted in any form or by any means, electronic, mechanical, photocopying, recording, or otherwise, without prior written permission of the author.

JOURNEYS OF EAGLES WHO SOAR
An Anthology Project
Volumn II

Eagles International Training Institute
P.O. Box 5667
Frisco, Texas 75035

ISBN 978-1-949027-08-2
Printed in the USA.
All rights reserved

Published by: Destined To Publish | Flossmoor, Illinois
www.DestinedToPublish.com

TABLE OF CONTENTS

20 Years and Beyond 1
    Dr. Pamela Scott

From Stuck to Unstoppable 12
    Dr. Irene Abrons

Lessons from the Eagle's Journey 19
    Marilyn Alexander

Fruitfull Barren Woman™: Embracing Purpose
Without Children, Soaring Without Limits 27
    Dr. Kina Arnold

Removing the MASK for the Journey 34
    Leslie Billups

Soaring To God's Purpose 44
    Tammy Chambers

The Weight of Yes 51
    S. Dee Clark-Riley

From Scarcity to Abundance:
   My Journey to Success and Financial Freedom........64
   Ingrid Conliffe-Easton

The Power of Waiting!............................75
   Janine Dailey

His Royal Diadem................................83
   Chiquista Dornell

Connecting In Spirit.............................95
   Dr. Charisse R. Drakeford

The Altar Where My Dance Began:
   The Altar Where My Dance Belongs...............101
   Gina M. Emanuel-Satchell

Serving to Soar.................................112
   Consuelo Gaines

Crossing Over...................................122
   Tomasito Gibbs

Trials to Triumphs: The Untold Lessons..............131
   Tesha Hall

I Spoke To You: Before I Formed You................141
   Melissa Hardy

From the Dance to the Nations......................154
   Janelle L. Jagdeo

The Door and the Flame:
   A Reflection of Surrender and Restoration..........166
   Leslyn A. Johnson

The Wonder of an Eagle's Growth...................189
   Jasmine La Rue

Hell Is Mad 198
    TYE MACK

In The Beginning 208
    TONYA R. MCCLURE

The Unfolding Majesty 218
    REVONDA A. MCKNIGHT, M.ED

Your Rise To Soar Is No Accident:
    It's Intentional, Desirable, And Fortunate! 229
    SENTHEIA MCLEOD

Divine Date of Destiny 239
    RENATE MCWRIGHT

Running With the Horses:
    Learn to T.A.P. and Go Higher 246
    LAWRENCE AND TAMARA NICHOLS

My Worship Is For Real 258
    YVONNE PAYNE

The Mouth Speaks 270
    STEPHANIE VANN

Becoming Me: A Worship Warrior's Journey 279
    JAMITA WRIGHT

20 YEARS AND BEYOND

I will never forget when God spoke to me as I was traveling on a plane. God called me to the nations years before the call for the school was released from His heart.

On this particular day, He clearly said to me, "Start the School." I had no idea what school He was referring to. I had been serving as the USA leader of another international ministry network, but He made it clear that the change in seasons had arrived.

At that point, I had a choice. Believe, obey, and move forward by faith or fear the unknown. I chose the former. I was taught that it is always better to trust and obey.

So I am here to encourage the reader, just like Mary the mother of Jesus did in John 2:5 (NASB) to the servants who asked for wine at the wedding in Cana. She said, *"Whatever He tells you, do it."*

20 Years! What have I learned? Trust and obey!

1. Just as the servants at the wedding in Cana did not know that their obedience would be the first of many miracles performed

by Jesus, I did not know that my obedience would result in many changed hearts and lives around the world.

When God speaks, we must be quick to listen and quick to obey. One of my favorite scriptures, found in Proverbs 8:34-35 (NASB), reads, *"Blessed is the man who listens to me, Watching daily at my gates, Waiting at my doorposts. For one who finds me finds life and obtains favor from the LORD."*

To listen to the Lord means to hear intelligently with obedience. It means to submit to what you have heard and walk in obedience by being a doer of what was spoken.

The call to obedience is the willingness to follow the Lord, even when you don't understand His instructions. That is why the scripture tells us in Romans 1:17b (NKJV), *"The just shall live by faith."*

As I trusted God, kept my eyes on Him, and walked in obedience to the word the Lord spoke to me in 2005, the school He spoke to me about on that plane was birthed. Now we are celebrating our 20th year, only by the grace of God.

When we walk in obedience to God, His proposals for us will prevail. We read in Deuteronomy 28:1 (NLT), *"If you fully obey the Lord your God and carefully keep all his commands that I am giving you today, the Lord your God will set you high above all the nations of the world."*

The promise given to me regarding the school from its inception can be found in Genesis 12:2-3 (NKJV), where God said to Abram, *"I will make you a great nation;*

I will bless you and make your name great; And you shall be a blessing. I will bless those who bless you, and I will curse him who curses you; And in you all the families of the earth shall be blessed."

As we began to grow, the Lord began to gather His ecclesia for kingdom purposes. Today, God allows us to train and equip the saints in over 25 nations. Obedience is a key that allows us access to God's favor but also to the overflow.

Over the years, I have learned that it is necessary to build on a solid foundation of the Word of God. We each have a blueprint given to us by the Lord. Obedience to His blueprint is what will lead us into victory.

1 Corinthians 3:12 tells us that each individual's work built upon the foundation of Jesus Christ will be revealed and tested by fire to determine if it will stand the test of time; therefore, we are encouraged to build wisely.

For me, building wisely means continuing to trust and obey daily and keep my ear on the heart of God.

"Know this, my beloved brothers: let every person be quick to hear, slow to speak, slow to anger; for the anger of man does not produce the righteousness of God" (James 1:19-20 ESV).

Though many obstacles have come to try to discourage me, I have learned that building wisely means being quick to forgive others who tried to harm me. *"Looking diligently lest any man fail of the grace of God; lest any root of bitterness springing up trouble you, and thereby many be defiled"* (Hebrews 12:15 KJV).

I refuse to hold on to unforgiveness. Unforgiveness can cause bitterness to take root within you. This can cause resentment, anger, or a long list of other negative emotions to arise, which will stifle you and stop your forward movement. Remember, this is a trick of the enemy. Don't fall for his tricks.

When you build according to the heart of God, He will bring others to stand with you. Just ask Nehemiah. The naysayers will be there, but you will be able to say, as Nehemiah did, that this work was accomplished only by the supernatural speed of the Holy Spirit.

As you read through the story of Nehemiah, you will discover that the walls of Jerusalem had been torn down for over 100 years. Others had tried to build it but were not successful. But when the call of God came to Nehemiah, the wall was finished in 52 days. It was a miracle. Part of his mandate was to restore and rebuild the literal walls of the city. Our mandate includes rebuilding the lives of those God brings to our school from the rubble of their mistakes. By His grace, we help to restore identity, hope, and purpose.

Be not discouraged. Trust and obey. As it admonishes us in Proverbs 3:5-6 (NKJV), *"Trust in the Lord with all your heart, And lean not on your own understanding; In all your ways acknowledge Him, and He shall direct your paths."*

He *shall* direct your path, not He *might* … He *shall!* And He did just that for us.

2. What have we done? We have spread our wings and soared on the word He spoke to me.

   Since our inception, we have grown into an established, accredited institute with a history of equipping the saints with a spirit of excellence. As the word says in Matthew 7:20 (NKJV), *"By their fruits you shall know them."*

   We began with a course to equip ministers of dance, with 30 ministers graduating in our first class. Since then, we have added over 20 courses, which include courses in English, Spanish, Dutch, and Korean. God has expanded our reach into the Spanish-speaking nations throughout the Caribbean and Europe.

   We now serve through our School of the Arts, School of Business, and School of Theology. We also serve the Body of Christ through our two-year doctoral program, where students can receive a DMin in Worship Arts, Dance Ministry, or Biblical Studies.

   What have we done? We have pioneered something that did not exist before. We were the first online equipping school of its kind. We have progressed from being a training school to being an apostolic training network.

   For 20 years, I have been aligned with Apostle Chuck Pierce at Glory of Zion International. The teaching I received over the years has not only changed my life but also changed those God has brought and continues to bring to the Eagles International Training Institute (EITI) and The Eagles Network (TEN). We now have a vibrant and passionate team of called and anointed leaders who serve with humility and soar with excellence.

I learned that we are living in a season of restoration. God has restored the offices of the fivefold ministry gifts as listed in Ephesians 4:11-12. This includes the Prophet and the Apostle.

Apostle means one who is sent. God sends us to establish His kingdom in the nations of the earth. God also instructed me while traveling on a ministry assignment, yes on a plane again, to send the graduates into their territory to teach on-site courses.

The EITI is online, so anyone can join from around the world. TEN is on-site and is able to equip hands-on, boots on the ground.

God desired to do new things so He sent us to pioneer what was in His heart for the nations.

What have we done?

- Through both the EITI and TEN, we have invaded and possessed new territory—naturally and spiritually.
- We have released and established worship that penetrates darkness to speak life and release light that leads people to freedom.
- We have been sent into the nations as pathfinders to open the way for others.
- We have motivated and pushed God's people forward.
- We have initiated new movements and succeeded in the face of overwhelming odds.

- We have been misunderstood, mistreated, and misquoted, and we have faced many obstacles, but we continue to press forward with courage, knowing the assignment we have been given.
- We have been sent into the nations for such a time as this.
- We have allowed God to lead us into paths of righteousness for His name's sake to equip the saints for the work of the ministry.

3. Where are we going, and what are we going to do?
    - We have been anointed with the spirit of the reformer to change nations. Reformers bring change to every situation in order to improve it. Therefore, we will continue to go as He sends us.
    - As reformers, we will continue to soar with boldness and love through every door God opens for us.
    - As reformers, we will continue to go into new territories to establish and build the Kingdom of God.
    - We will continue to help raise up leaders after God's heart.
    - As reformers, we will continue to take the Good News of the Gospel to those crying in the wilderness.

I like to say that when Jesus came, He brought the power of the Kingdom of Heaven. He did not bring a dead religion with no power. Therefore, He does not want us to be in bondage to anyone, at any time, for any reason. He brought us the message of love and freedom!

- As reformers, we will not be afraid to face existing religious structures or old systems that stand against any new thing God wants to do and establish.

- As reformers, we will continue to move beyond the cultural and social norms of society.

- As reformers, we will continue to soar with an end-times apostolic and prophetic anointing to shake nations.

It will take the end-times anointing to penetrate the darkness that is around us.

Isaiah 8:18 (NKJV) says, *"Here am I and the children whom the Lord has given me! We are for signs and wonders in Israel From the Lord of hosts, Who dwells in Mount Zion."*

We will be His signs and wonders on Earth. We were not meant just to warm a pew Sunday after Sunday. We were meant to be bright and conspicuous as we shine bright for Jesus in a dark world.

What are we going to do?

- We will continue to herald a clarion call to the Bride of Christ in this season to rise from slumber into a glorious Church that moves in the same miracles Jesus did.

  It is clear there is a great harvest of souls coming in. This harvest will be brought in by a supernatural generation that has been thoroughly prepared for harvest.

- We will be harvesters to help bring in the precious fruit of the earth.

- We will do the same works that Jesus did and greater works.

John 20:21 (BRG) reads, *"Then said Jesus to them again, Peace be unto you: as my Father hath sent me, even so send I you."*

- We will say yes to wherever God wants to send us to establish His kingdom in every sphere of society. We are the only hope for a hopeless world.

The world is waiting for us! They are waiting for EAGLES and for TEN.

Why? *"... as He is, so are we in this world"* (1 John 4:17 NKJV).

We are those who will see His will become a reality on Earth.

Everywhere Jesus went, He interrupted systems.

He interrupted sickness.

He interrupted lack.

He interrupted fear.

He interrupted old seasons.

He interrupted old thought processes.

JESUS interrupted every system and established kingdom.

He interrupted the sin structure of man.

Jesus interrupted every old religious paradigm. He interrupted every plan of the enemy. This is what we are also called to do.

God has chosen us to be part of His apostolic, end-time ecclesia that has so much power that even the gates of hell cannot prevail against us, and no weapon formed against us will prosper.

God has graced us to serve and soar, equipping the saints for 20 years. This is only the beginning.

- We will remain resilient.
- We will endure.
- We will set our face like a flint and put our hands and hearts to the work He has assigned to us.

God is building a strong tribe, and many will come to be part of this family. We will be ready to receive them.

Together, we will bring light where there is presently darkness and carry salvation to the ends of the earth.

How will we transform nations?

- Through prayer and fasting. Both are foundational to changing a nation.
- Through the sound teaching of the Word of God. We will not compromise.
- Through evangelism. We will be Jesus everywhere we go.
- Through living in unity. Psalm 133 tells us that where there is unity, God gives a charge, sends, and commands the blessing.
- "Bless those who persecute you; bless and do not curse them" (Romans 12:14 ESV).
- Through love and forgiveness. John 3:16 (NKJV) states: "For God so loved the world that He gave His only begotten Son, that whoever believes in Him should not perish but have everlasting life."

- We will love one another with brotherly affection and outdo one another in showing honor (Romans 12:10).

- We will live in harmony with one another. We will not be haughty, but we will associate with the lowly (Romans 12:16).

- We will not repay evil for evil but give thought to do what is honorable in the sight of all (Romans 12:17).

- We will continue to walk by faith! Faith operates by His love. Faith prevails through His love. Faith is active through His love. Faith is powerful through His love.

- We say yes. We will be reformers of every sphere over which we have been given influence.

Father, we say that we love You because You first loved us, and by Your grace we will love others with Your love that we may see a mighty revival in the nations of the earth. We will continue to be the voice of those crying in the wilderness. We will leave a heritage for others to follow by continuing to develop a rich spiritual legacy for those who will come after us.

Here we are. Send us!

FROM STUCK TO UNSTOPPABLE

When Life Stalls

There was a season in my life where I felt completely and utterly stuck. My mind was clouded with self-doubt. I had gained a significant amount of weight, and my skin was breaking out in painful, persistent acne. My self-esteem was at an all-time low. I honestly felt hopeless. I didn't recognize the woman staring back at me in the mirror. I felt stuck.

But God.

I am so grateful to Him for His grace and mercy. He sent me people who ministered to me, came alongside me, and helped me birth something new. I began to experience a shift—a new mindset, a new lease on life, a renewed purpose. And I made a decision: I will not go back.

The Hidden Signs of Being Stuck

All my life, the enemy tried to keep me locked in the cycle of depression and isolation. I never quite felt like I fit in. That sense of not belonging became fertile ground for the enemy's lies, keeping me stuck and stagnant. But God, in His infinite wisdom and love, was writing a different story for me a story of breakthrough, freedom, and destiny.

Identifying the signs of being stuck is the first step toward change. For professional women, especially those of faith, these signs often show up as frustration, fatigue, or the quiet resignation that comes when our dreams feel too far away. If you find yourself consistently dissatisfied in your work, your relationships, or your spiritual life, it's time to pause and reflect. God didn't design you to live in perpetual frustration. You were created for more.

One major sign of being stuck is a nagging dissatisfaction with your accomplishments. Maybe you scroll through social media, feeling envy rise up as others celebrate their wins. Maybe you feel your energy slipping away as you dread going to work, attending meetings, or starting yet another project that feels meaningless. That lack of motivation may not just be laziness—it could be divine discontent. God could be stirring your spirit because He has something more aligned with your purpose.

Another sign is the feeling of being overwhelmed. When everything feels like too much, we tend to procrastinate or shut down. This cycle of stress and avoidance only deepens the pit of stagnation. But God's Word offers a remedy: "My grace is sufficient for you, for My power is made perfect in weakness" (2 Corinthians 12:9). We're not meant to carry the weight alone.

Stagnation often shows up as a lack of growth. Whether you're no longer learning at your job or feeling spiritually dry, you might be stuck in a comfort zone that no longer serves you. Proverbs 1:5 says, "Let the wise listen and add to their learning." Growth requires intention and often a leap of faith.

Sometimes, being stuck reveals itself through a spiritual disconnect. When prayer, worship, and fellowship become afterthoughts instead of lifelines, we drift into survival mode. But we were never meant to survive we were created to thrive. John 10:10 says, "I have come that they may have life, and have it to the full." Your spiritual vitality is essential for moving forward.

The Shift: When God Redirects

The emotional toll of stagnation can be intense. Professional women carry multiple roles, and when progress stalls, it can feel like a personal failure. The weight of expectations our own and others' can crush our confidence. This often leads to feelings of inadequacy, shame, and isolation. But the truth is, your value doesn't decrease in seasons of struggle. In fact, these seasons can become your most fruitful when you lean into God.

I remember that season all too well. I was serving as an operational manager in a role I had no passion for. My body was crying out I was anemic, constantly needing blood transfusions, and emotionally depleted. I was also trying to finish my doctorate while navigating difficult decisions about starting a family. I was exhausted.

Then God did what only He could do: He closed the door.

I was laid off—suddenly and without warning. One moment, I was preparing to solidify my career as an Operations and Project Manager. I was studying for the PMP exam, ready to dig deep and commit fully to what I believed was my long-term path. I had plans, strategy, and vision.

But then came the unexpected disruption.

Not only was I released from the position—I was the one who trained my replacement. Talk about a blow to the heart. It felt like rejection. It felt unfair. It felt like the ground beneath me had crumbled.

But what looked like rejection… was actually divine redirection.

God was shifting the soil beneath my feet, not to bury me, but to plant me in purpose. Isaiah 55:8-9 reminds us, *"For my thoughts are not your thoughts, neither are your ways my ways," declares the Lord.* And oh, how true that became in my life.

That unexpected transition became the doorway to destiny. That season of shaking became the launching pad of my purpose. I went on my first dance mission trip, and it lit a fire within me I didn't know existed. Since then, by God's grace, I've ministered across 8 nations on 3 continents dancing prophetically, worshiping freely, and witnessing breakthrough around the world.

God opened a door in higher education, and I walked through it with boldness. Today, I serve as a College Professor and the Dean of Student Affairs. My body, once weary and worn, began to heal. I stopped merely surviving and started to thrive.

I launched my own business. I host a powerful podcast that's blessing lives. My life is a living testimony that what the enemy meant for evil, God has used for good (Genesis 50:20).

He did it before and I know He'll do it again.

This journey taught me to lean in, to trust not in titles or timelines, but in the One who orders every step. *"Trust in the Lord with all your heart and lean not on your own understanding; in all your ways acknowledge Him, and He will direct your path"* (Proverbs 3:5-6).

Glory to God. He did it all. And He's not finished yet.

The Path Forward

Moving forward is both a decision and a process. Philippians 3:13-14 says, "Forgetting what is behind and straining toward what is ahead, I press on." Forward motion starts with clarity. Ask God to reveal His plan. You don't need to know every step—just the next one. Proverbs 3:5-6 reminds us that He will direct our paths when we trust Him.

Next, make the decision to release the past. Isaiah 43:18-19 tells us, "Forget the former things... I am doing a new thing!" That new thing requires new faith. You can't walk into a new season with an old mindset.

Then comes action. Faith without works is dead. Start the business. Apply for the job. Join the ministry. Take the class. God honors motion.

And finally, trust the process. Growth is rarely linear. There will be setbacks, but God promises in Romans 8:28 that all things will work together for your good. Surround yourself with people who speak life and truth. Proverbs 27:17 says, "As iron sharpens iron, so one person sharpens another."

Today, I walk in a freedom I once thought was impossible. I've released the shame of my past. I've embraced the healing of my present. And I've committed to the purpose of my future.

You, too, can move from stuck to unstoppable. Through God's grace, the power of community, and your own resilience, you can rise. God is not finished with you. Your story is still being written. And the next chapter? It's going to be powerful.

From Survival to Soaring

Let's go. Let's rise. Let's move forward, unstoppable.

Reflection: What's one area of your life where you feel stuck? What might God be inviting you to release?

Prayer: Father, I surrender every area of my life that feels stuck. I give You my disappointments, my fears, and my confusion. Replace them with Your clarity, peace, and purpose. Help me to release what no longer serves me and embrace the new thing You are doing in me. I trust You to guide me, strengthen me, and restore me. In Jesus' name, Amen.

ABOUT THE AUTHOR

Dr. Irene M. Abrons is a published author of several books and academic journals. With over 25 years of experience, she empowers leaders through entrepreneurship training and strategic coaching. As co-founder of Abrons Next Level Coaching, she helps organizations grow with purpose, excellence, and measurable impact.

LESSONS FROM THE EAGLE'S JOURNEY

Recently I've discovered a new fascination for eagles. These birds are both majestic and beautiful, and they soar higher than any other bird on the planet. For me, the eagle and its journey mirror so much of what I feel life is like. Life isn't easy. It's filled with high moments and setbacks. But, like the eagle, we are built to soar, not stay grounded.

I didn't know until recently that the crow is really the only natural enemy of the eagle and the only bird bold enough to attack it. Think about that for a second. The crow is both smaller and weaker and is no match for the eagle's strength or its wingspan. Yet it still dares to land on the eagle's back and peck at its neck.

If that's not life, I don't know what is. Haven't you ever felt that way? You know the strength and potential that you carry inside. And here comes some crow, some distraction, some critic, some problem, that perches on your back and starts pecking. It causes you to doubt every promise God ever gave to you.

But here's something to think about: the eagle doesn't waste time or energy wrestling with crows. It doesn't even turn around to fight the crow. It simply rises higher. The eagle soars to altitudes where the crow can't breathe until eventually it suffocates and falls off.

I've had many crows in my life. There have been times when people criticized me unfairly, when setbacks showed up back-to-back, and when distractions felt relentless. Seasons where I thought I had to prove myself, so I kept saying yes. But instead of soaring, I felt weighed down. These are times when everything feels like pecks, and every peck adds up. Had I looked at things through the eyes of an eagle, I would have realized that I was wasting energy dealing with things that were beneath me.

So, that's the first lesson the eagle has taught me: stop letting small things steal my energy. We don't have to answer every critic or wrestle with every distraction. Sometimes the best answer is simply to rise higher.

Now, a truth we don't like to admit is that sometimes the crow isn't on the outside. Sometimes the crow is us! The crow is our own voice of doubt, our fear, and, for me, procrastination. I've had seasons when no one else had to tell me I couldn't do something because I was doing a fine job of sabotaging myself, all by myself. But the solution wasn't to flap my wings harder or give in to my own insecurities. The solution was to soar so high that self-sabotaging would have to drop off because of the altitude. I know it might be easier said than done, but the 'God' thing is that it *can* be done!

I've seen this with the writers I've coached. Many authors find themselves as the crow of their own story. They come to us timid and unsure if their story mattered. Some didn't even think they had a story. I've watched men and women alike stare at a blank page, convinced they had nothing to say, and discover that the very things they thought were ordinary were extraordinary and held dynamic impact.

What I have learned in 20 years of publishing is that if authors are offered encouragement and accountability, they reveal the eagle within themselves! And when they finally shared the words they thought weren't good enough, we visibly saw healing in their eyes. What I love most about what I do is that it is never just about writing a book. It's always about helping an author realize that their voice matters. I've said it for too many years: someone on the other side is waiting to hear your story! Because seeing an eagle soar reminds us that we were also meant to soar! I've seen the moment when an author realizes their journey can become someone else's roadmap to flight, and in that moment, it is like watching an eagle lock its eyes forward. And when that spark of something they thought was unattainable suddenly feels within reach, you can almost see them take flight because they are no longer focused on the crow.

It is my prayer as a publisher that every person realizes that writing is about legacy! Your story is the act of leaving a mark on the world that cannot be erased, the same way an eagle leaves its shadow as it soars across the sky. Some writers have published multiple books. Others wrote one story that changed the way their children and grandchildren saw them. I have seen authors discover a confidence they didn't know they had, not just on the page but in their everyday lives. And I've also watched other authors begin teaching and inspiring others because they now understood the power of their own journey and their own testimony. Just like eagles that ride a current, their words are carried farther because they lift up others along the way. There is a ripple effect in a story. It doesn't stop with the author; it moves and it multiplies. There is revelation in knowing that you can't leave enough possessions to build a legacy. Legacy is not found in your title, and the Bible warns us against the applause of men. Legacy is the imprint of your life that lives on in someone else. It is the faith that you leave behind.

There comes a time in the journey of every eagle when it must go through a renewal season. And what amazes me most is the resilience it shows during this painful process. At the midpoint in an eagle's life, its long, sharp beak begins to bend and become brittle, its talons curl so it can no longer grab prey, and its wings are worn, weighed down, and so heavy that it is difficult to fly.

At this point, the eagle looks vulnerable and weak, almost like it couldn't survive another fight. And if I'm honest, I've felt that way too. Years of struggling through can wear you down until it feels like you don't have the strength to go on another day. But this is the moment when the eagle faces two choices: die or go through the painful process of change.

So the eagle retreats to a hiding place at the top of a high mountain and begins the most painful transformation process of its life. Imagine having to strike its beak against a rock so hard and so many times that it breaks off. Once the new beak grows in, imagine having to pluck its talons from its feet one by one. And still after the talons regrow, imagine having to pluck every feather from its body. Imagine that the very tools you have used for survival must be surrendered and painfully destroyed.

I think it is an understatement to say that this rebirthing season is not easy. It is unimaginably painful and lonely but also necessary. And if we don't allow ourselves to go through these painful seasons of letting go and renewal, we risk never becoming what we were created to be. The eagle endures all this pain because it knows there is more life ahead. And there is so much life ahead for us too. Just like the eagle hides away in the cleft of the mountain, God pulls us under His wing and allows us to be renewed.

Personally, I feel like I'm emerging from my own renewing season. Maybe you are too. During that time, it felt like everything fell apart all at once. I didn't feel strong. I felt stripped of everything I thought made me who I was. The relationship I believed would last forever began to unravel and break my trust. It broke my spirit, but for the grace of God, it would have broken me. Retreating didn't feel like soaring; it felt like failing. I had poured my heart into this relationship, believing it was secure, but I watched it collapse. And when it was gone, I didn't know who I was without it.

But here's what I see now, that time of being hidden away was not wasted. It was necessary. I had to shed what no longer served me. I had to let go of parts of myself that were dull and heavy. And yes, it was painful, and at times, it still is. But I know now that without that process, I could not have been renewed.

So, I can now put all this into perspective with Psalm 103:5: 'Our youth is renewed like the eagle's.' Just like the eagle, I had to choose to do the hard work, or else I would not have survived. But unlike the eagle, I didn't have to go through this painful process alone. In fact, I didn't even have to do it myself. The Lord promises that HE will renew us like the eagle.

These seasons of renewal can be brutal, but they are also beautiful. Because in that hidden place, the eagle regrows feathers, sharpens its talons, and grows a new beak. When it finally emerges, the eagle takes what is called "the famous flight of rebirth," and it soars higher and stronger than ever before and lives for another thirty years!

I think sometimes we pay more attention to our hits than our wins. I know sometimes I do. We obsess over who criticized us, who left us, what we lost, where we failed, or who failed us. And in doing so, we miss the doors opening right in front of us. I've been guilty of this. There have been times when one negative comment overshadowed ten people's encouragement. Times when one setback made me blind to the opportunities that were still alive. I think that's why I love the image of the eagle so much now. It doesn't waste time looking back. Its eyes are fixed forward. Its vision is laser sharp, able to spot prey miles away. If I'm being honest, I've had to remind myself to stop counting the crows and start spotting the opportunities.

There was a time when I held on to disappointment so tightly that I almost missed open doors right in front of me. A mentor reached out with an opportunity, but I was so wrapped up in what had gone wrong that I almost said no; in fact, I think originally, I did say no. But thankfully, I eventually said yes. And that yes opened my eyes to see things I didn't know were there and the ripple effect of lives being changed and healed. My setbacks remind me that my story is not over, they just mean the next chapter is waiting. And the eagle reminds me that where you fix your eyes matters. If you only focus on the loss, you'll miss the gain. If you only look at what's gone, you'll miss what's coming.

And then there's the lesson of community. Eagles are often seen as solitary, but they also thrive in community, especially when raising their young. And isn't that life too? We may think we're strong enough to go it alone, but we need community. We need people to challenge and remind us that we were made for more. I've been blessed to dwell in that kind of community, but I'll be the first to admit: as an only child, it hasn't always been easy. Being in community means being stretched. It means hearing the truth when you don't want to. It means being called higher when you'd rather stay comfortable. But what I have learned is that it's worth it! Because without community, we might not soar as high as we were meant to.

A saying that I adopted over 20 years ago is this: "Everyone has a story—something to reveal, something to teach, something to inspire. You are not just a writer, you are an inspiration. And because every story needs a reader, every story must be shared. It may not be in the traditional sense of cover and pages, but it may be passed down in family conversations. However it is told, every story matters, and every story will leave something behind."

So, I've said all of this to say, soaring isn't optional...legacy isn't optional. Legacy is the imprint we make on the earth. I am so excited to be a part of this anthology because it is filled with stories of legacy. Stories of Eagles who have gone through a rebirthing process of their own and have come out soaring! And I am excited to know that we are all on the tip of something deeper. Because every chapter represents someone's flight. I have read these stories and have felt the wind of inspiration. I pray that others who read these pages will be encouraged to soar also.

ABOUT THE AUTHOR

Marilyn Alexander is in her seventh year as the Eagles Authors Instructor and is the founder of *Destined to Publish*, an independent hybrid publishing company helping authors leave lasting legacies. A passionate mentor and coach, Marilyn believes every voice matters. She treasures being mother to two children who inspire her journey of faith and purpose.

FRUITFULL BARREN WOMAN™: EMBRACING PURPOSE WITHOUT CHILDREN, SOARING WITHOUT LIMITS

In the beginning...

I always believed that when you live a life in right standing before the Father, all things are possible in the life He provides for you. Each breath is a moment that cannot be duplicated or repeated. Yes, God is the redeemer of time. Nevertheless, we must seize each moment as if it were our last, with complete abandonment of the fear of failure.

Failure is nothing but life lessons for the step that you are on and the moment you are living in. Those lessons are priceless because they teach you an inner strength that can never be replaced with a false identity. In those vulnerable spaces, you learn who you are and what treasures are inside of you for your next move. It is called grounded development instead of arrested development.

There is nothing you cannot accomplish when you truly know the hidden treasures inside of you that require excavation through the Holy Spirit.

Barrenness Reimagined...

To be barren means one who is unproductive and has no contribution worthy of consideration. On the contrary, to be fruitful is a celebration of the ripeness of the fruit and seeds that are borne from the pressure of cultivation, the struggle to be valued, and the fight to thrive.

Being barren is no easy journey. In fact, between 2015–2019, over 13% of women between the ages of 15–49 experienced some portion of infertility (NationalHealthStatisticsReport.com). It's a blessed anointing while at the same time it's a cursed word. Blessings include being able to come and go as you please, no one to take care of except yourself, and being just free from "little human" responsibilities. Running simultaneously is the curse—that the world finds you defective, needing repair, lonely, and automatically a modern-day feminist.

Well, I am neither the world's definition of blessed, nor its casual branding of cursed.

I am a fruitfull barren woman who has produced more than I could have ever borne through my body. Scripture tells the barren woman to enlarge her tent and stabilize her tent pegs because the persons within her tent far exceed her infantile understanding (Isaiah 54:1).

The Sting of the timeless question...

"When are you having children?" is a question that has clouded my life for over 30 years—especially after I married in 2010, to the one who was prepared for me by ABBA. After three failed engagements, I finally followed YAH's leading and wedded my forever love. I am Big G's rib that was formed from him for him.

Even walking through marital counseling with my love was taxing for some of the counselors who failed to understand our complete surrender to YAH's direction when it came to having naturally born children or adopted children or even consideration of surrogacy. Whatever YAH's divine desires for us as a Kingdom power couple was—and still is—well with our soul. That is the pressure: to patiently wait for HIS direction and still live fulfilled lives, living in the present and not focusing on what the future may hold for us. Yet still in the back of my mind is an ache for motherhood that has not been satisfied. And likely, it will never be in the natural.

Cultivating the foundation for our seeds in the spirit to manifest in the natural world has been quite difficult. Knowing that my body does not reproduce after its own kind, even with the help of extensive fertility treatment, was—and I will admit—still is heartbreaking especially seeing it work divinely for others. I am neither the world's definition of blessed, nor its casual conversation of cursed. I am phenomenally and supernaturally fruitfuLL in many ways that has left me in awe and left others perplexed.

My Biblical Identity...

I compare myself to Sarai, who laughed at the thought of having a baby past menopause's silence (Genesis 18:12–15). I even looked just like my sistah Hannah, who cried out to the Lord for help and made promises of dedication of her seed for HIS glory (1 Samuel 2). Yep, I made those promises too. Unlike Hannah, nothing happened for me. Then there was sweet Elizabeth (Luke 1:23-25), who had dedicated herself to the Lord's work only to lose him as a young adult for the cause of the Kingdom (Mark 6:14-29). I thought about whether I could bear the pain of becoming pregnant and miscarrying, or the baby having medically incurable complexities, or even dying tragically sometime after birth. As I pondered, barrenness was not so bad after all.

So, if I am not fruitful physically, how else can I be fruitful? And that is when it hit me like an asteroid from Heaven's Throne Room: Some barren women are equipped to bear children; however, their yes to God required a sacrifice of the productivity of their womb.

Saying it another way—barren women are fruitful in wisdom, love, endurance, patience, compassion, encouragement, and longevity. Hence, a fruitfuLL barren woman™ is a conduit for HIS heart to pour into disposable children, youth, and young adults who are tragically in need of HIS pour. You see, God uses the womb of the fruitfuLL barren woman™ to be a reservoir of eternal hope, rooted wisdom, and uncomplicated love for all those in need.

If you think that you are her, then you and me are the same. You are me, and I am you.

My Tent is BEcoming full...

So, as we move through life without biological children, our arms are stretched wide, our tents are busting at the seams for the people that God has entrusted us to pour into daily. We replicate after HIS kind—supernaturally and authentically. What greater example than Jesus – Yeshua Himself that never married or had a child from his loins. Yet, we are born through and in Him as HIS siblings (Galatians 4:5), HIS co-heirs (Romans 8:17), HIS friends (John 15:15), and HIS disciples (John 12:26). He is also our Savior (Jude 1:25), Redeemer (Romans 3:23-24), and our King (Revelations 17:14, 19:16). Jesus is all of these and so much more. He chose me to be just as I am in the Earth, so HIS Glory shines through my personal struggle by HIS grace. This is the thorn in my side which may be different than the Apostle Paul. Nevertheless, HIS grace is truly sufficient (2 Corinthians 12:9).

It's with intentionality we create businesses, write books, teach students, use our talents, invest our treasure, and prioritize our time—while on HIS potter's wheel for HIS molding by fire (Jeremiah 18:1–6). It is then The Great I AM shoots us out of HIS bow to a plethora of people and places (Isaiah 49:2). The fruitfulness of our lives returns to us in subtle ways that you will not immediately notice. You must recognize when they occur because these moments are life-giving. These treasured experiences are etched in time when you need them the most: when life is a tsunami of dried lemons. Yet, you press forward and upward with the spark that only HE can keep alive.

HIS Glory manifested exceptionally...

Make no mistake, we are wonderfully designed to do HIS Greater Works in this world (John 14:12). For we bear the mark of HIM who has called us—by embracing the barrenness of our condition—yet remaining ever committed to HIS calling to be fruitful and multiply (Genesis 1:28). We too are fruitful in HIS Kingdom from now until He returns. Be encouraged, my sistah, as you have your saddened moments of infertility. These moments are real, tangible, excruciating and hard. Don't ignore how you feel in those moments. Just know, they will pass as you cry to the Abba. He always hears and cares, even during those moments when it seems overwhelming. It is in those moments that you must raise HIS standard of grace to get up out of your depressed bed and find joy in the fruit you have bore.

Our daily affirmation...

You are a fruitfuLL barren woman™ —born with great purpose, destined to soar! You feel pressure from the stretching of your tent. Don't fight it; flow in HIS Glory that is upon you and the bountiful works of your hands. There is so much for you to say. There is so much for you to do. Let's go in HIS power, my Sistah with every ounce of strength because HE has greater work for us to do. I will see you in the trenches…Kina.

> *"Rejoice, O barren, You who do not bear!*
> *Break forth and shout, You who are not in labor!*
> *For the desolate has many more children*
> *Than she who has a husband."*
>
> **—Galatians 4:27, NKJV**

ABOUT THE AUTHOR

 Dr. Kina Arnold is a licensed minister, inspirational speaker, and founder of YAHWEH Beaute' Inc., PURe Beaute' Inc, and Reigning INside OUT! LLC. She empowers women and youth through Biblical instruction and personal development. Kina is the author of The Priesthood of the Dance, HIS Bride, See Me and Verme'.

REMOVING THE MASK FOR THE JOURNEY

WHAT ARE YOU MASKING?

MASK, according to the web, is a covering for all or part of the face. The MASK can be worn as a disguise. It is also a covering that is made from fiber or gauze and created to fit over the nose and mouth to protect against dust, air pollutants, and any other foreign substances.

In 2020, life as we knew it took a turn for the entire world. We fell into a place where there was a pandemic so big that it caused us to change the appearance of ourselves whenever we had to go outside and when we had to be around other people. This major change was the use of the MASK. During that time, there were so many different styles and types of masks that were created for people to wear. We had cloth masks that were equipped for the everyday community of people. There were surgical masks, N95 respirator masks, and KN95 respirator masks that were equipped for our community of essential workers and first responders. Then we have Jabbawockeez Masks for our community of actors. So many types of masks that were created for various purposes.

While researching, I found something very interesting about the masks that are used by essential workers and first responders. Something that stood out to me was the letters that have been strategically pulled to indicate the different types of surgical masks: N, R, and P. For the masks that were labeled with the letter N, these masks were *"not resistant to oil."* For the masks that were labeled with the letter R, these masks had *"some resistance to oil."* For the masks that were labeled with the letter P, these masks were *"strongly resistant to oil."* WOW, this right here, because when we think about the OIL of the Holy Spirit, we know that to be a representation of the power and the presence, the healing and deliverance, and a cleansing: all things needed to UnMask the Mask of Life!

In life, we often put on a mask and attempt to wear it well. We can wear the MASK to a masquerade ball. We can wear the MASK while in "lights, camera, action" mode. We can even wear the MASK in particular sports that require the use of a face MASK. But when we stop and take a deeper look at the MASK and how it is demonstrated in these entities, we find that the commonality is being hidden for a moment. At a masquerade event, one would use the MASK to hide or disguise one's true identity. One can portray, as actors and actresses, someone whom they really are not. In the sports world, football

players wear the face MASK to block and protect their faces during the games. So the question is: "Why do YOU wear the MASK?"

THE MIME AND THE MOVEMENT

As I pondered and even processed this question for myself, it took me back to my beginning years as I entered the world of mime. I first began the ministry of mime in 2008, and while in this early phase of the ministry, I knew that it was important for me to gather all of the information and knowledge that I needed for this art in order to become effective. Now, notice that I said I focused on gathering knowledge and understanding of the art; nowhere had I become concerned about the ME of mime. I knew that tapping into the ME of mime would require me to remove the MASK that I often wore so that I could understand who the ME was.

Through the years, I pushed myself in the area and ministry of movement because that was all that I knew of who Leslie was. I had become *"strongly resistant to the Oil (Holy Spirit)"* because I did not understand nor was I tapped into the Oil that resided inside of me. For nine years, I hid behind the mask of my own identity because all I knew was movement and how it got the attention of the people. So, as a result of me only identifying myself to the area of movement, that is what others had begun to see in me the most. But I knew that the day would come where I had to Remove the MASK for this Next Journey. I was nervous and all, but it was something that needed to be done.

The Year 2017 begun what was about to be the beginning of a life-changing journey for me. Not only was I nervous about what was getting ready to happen because I knew that what I was preparing to do was going to open up some doors for me, but also there were areas of increase in my life as I started the journey to full-time mime ministry. I had to now take this big leap into transitioning from what I thought I knew about mime to developing a deeper study of how to tap into the Authentic Me. This is when I now developed *"some resistance to the Oil (Holy Spirit)."* I knew that by taking this next step, everything from there was just going to keep going higher and higher. This marked a turning point, where I began to understand what it truly meant to soar and serve. "I was not ready" is what I kept telling myself. I had to remove the MASK that I had placed over myself all those years before and enter into the full journey into the TRUTH of mime.

THE SHIFT INTO VOICE

The year 2020 marked the path toward a new chapter as I now entered into a level where I absolutely had no idea that my voice mattered. This was the biggest challenge and largest mask that I ever had to remove in my life. I had to now come from behind the mask of movement to the frontline of speaking. This was huge because I absolutely hated speaking. I would only speak when I felt it was necessary. My safety blanket was silence, hence being a nonverbal communicator through mime. Not only was I hiding behind the paint and demonstrative movement, but I was also hiding behind Tourette Syndrome. I felt like I communicated better nonverbally as long as I did not have to speak. However, this was the year that the "Removing of the MASK for This Journey" became very real for me. I was invited to be the instructor for the EITI Mime Course, and it shook everything inside of me. I knew that I could not say no, because this movement of Mime Nation was deep inside of me. The idea of speaking not just to persons locally but to persons all over the world became more nerve-racking. I had shifted back into the place of being *"strongly resistant to the OIL"* because God was pulling on me to now step out of my comfort zone and into a place that I was already positioned and purposed for. All types of things began to run through my mind. I had become concerned about my verbal and nonverbal tics and what turn they would take. I was wearing a disguise because I did not want people to see the real me. The reality was that the real ME that I was hiding was the one who can speak! The one who can teach! The one who can build, equip, and lead! I was hiding that one! You see, I did not want people to know that I was capable of doing all of these things, yet I always had this idea in my head that the only thing I was anointed to do was minister the Word through movement. Removing the MASK for the Journey Ahead!

THE PAINT AND THE PURPOSE

The masquerade, the facade, the synthetic fabrics of what we paint life to be for us can ultimately become a huge downfall. So how do we Remove the MASK? To remove something means to get rid of it; to take it away. The Greek 525 terms *apo* and *allassó* mean to remove, to release, to depart, to be quit of one, to set free, and to deliver.

1 Corinthians 15:33 tells us we cannot be misled by the things of evil, and in the same way we cannot mislead the people through the false pretenses of what God has called us to do. We cannot continue to MASK life. We hear many expressions using the word "MASK": masking pain, masking hurt, masking disappointments and frustrations. But when we MASK those things, we are only

covering up and hiding the true feeling. The devil hides salvation because he is evil, but a believer should share salvation. What you try to hide behind the mask will eventually be revealed—once that mask is removed.

As a mime, one of the things that we learn, because we are storytellers, is that we absolutely cannot hide our faces and hide our feelings. Oftentimes as young children growing up, we may have heard our parents or guardians tell us not to cry or say that we could not show (demonstrate) facial expressions, when in fact our faces tell the greatest stories of all. But what story is your face telling? Looking at MASK, through masquerading, we tell stories of deception; through acting, we tell stories in our behavior; through the synthetics, we tell stories that are not real; and through knockoffs, we tend to copy the stories of others. Through all of these forms, the ultimate connection is that there is no authenticity coming from our stories. This is the season to Remove the MASK!

Here we have the MASK. The first and most important piece for creating this Worship MASK is as follows:

- The White Paint: This represents the purity that we have. As we are washed up clean and made whole, God creates within us a clean heart (Psalm 51:10). While we are daily removing the mask of evil, hatred, and discord, He is purifying us with the heart of Love. Before we go forth and do anything, we must first ask God to give us a clean heart so that what we present and minister to others is that which is not contrary to the Word of God.

- The Black for the Brows: They are drawn in place to enhance the expression. It is through the eyes that we have to Remove the Mask and shift from focusing on the things in the natural and begin to see what God is doing in the Spirit. We ask God to seal the eyes, closing them to the things of the world and opening them to the things of the Spirit (Proverbs 21:2-3).

- Nose: As we cover the nose with this beautiful white paint, we are removing the MASK and asking God to make us sensitive to the needs of the people. Allow us to minister to the heart of the people from a place of true and pure worship and not from the flesh. Be discerning of the things that are good and evil, being cautious not to release the evil (Proverbs 3:13).

- Mouth: As we seal the mouth, we pause and close it shut so that we are not speaking verbally. We are removing the MASK of death, curses, and blasphemy that can often come from the mouth. We are asking God to use our body to speak the message as we have totally submitted it unto Him (Proverbs 13:3)!

- The Circle: COMPLETION. Through God, all things are possible and complete! Without Him being the center of our lives, we cannot move forward. With this circle, as we close up and remove the excess paint that may be smeared, we are asking God to keep us together. Remove the MASK of isolation so that the Journey to Success and Healing can begin. There is no beginning, and there is no ending, only the fullness therein that builds more on the covenant relationship that one has with the Father (Colossians 2:10).

UNMASKING FOR THE JOURNEY AHEAD

Removing the MASK for the Next Journey in your life is a big step. While it can seem challenging and just totally out of the norm for some, it must be done. One will never truly understand the OIL that they carry. This is the time to come out of hiding and explore those things which God has placed in front of you. No more looking back and having second thoughts about whether you can do it or not.

If Glory Carriers is what God has called you to be—REMOVE THE MASK of Doubt!

If Planet Shaker is what God has called you to be—REMOVE THE MASK of Fear!

If Global Missions is what God has called you to—REMOVE THE MASK of Timidness!

Remove all of the MASKS so that you can Spread Your Wings and Soar High Into Your Next Journey!

UNMASK THE MASK TO YOUR LIFE!!!!

THE KINGDOM REDEFINES THE MASK

We can certainly turn this thing around, and while we are removing the MASK for the journey, let us pause for a moment and look at the MASK. When we think about a physical mask, some can be smooth and some can be a little rough where they have patterns on them. However, as I am a full-time Mime Worship artist, I want to share with you the behind-the-scenes aspect of the Mime Face and the White Paint and what it all means. To go Behind the Paint of the Worshipper and into the MASK below is a description and a breakdown of what we will see through the eyes of a mime. Now we can get to the root of the MASK and how to come from Behind the Mask for this next journey. It is almost not possible to stay stuck in a place, to stay in hiding because we become too afraid to step into the next place that God has already laid before us. The last four years have been strategic years, and I had no idea how strategic they were because I wanted to remain in hiding; I was not ready to remove the MASK so that I could now take this journey. We have to move away from *Masquerading Acting Synthetic Knockoffs* and into *Meritoriously Aligned (to) Serve (in the) Kingdom!*

REFLECTION PROMPT

Here are some reflection questions that I invite you to reflect upon concerning your own "mask" and some things that you may be hiding behind:

- What MASK are you wearing that God is asking you to remove?
- Where have you been resisting the oil of the Holy Spirit?
- Who are you when the paint comes off?

ABOUT THE AUTHOR

Leslie Billups is the founder of and visionary for D'Vyne Anointed Ministries and TEAM DYNOMIME, a virtual, in-depth, self-paced training course that will take all who desire mime through the many facets of what True Mime embodies, while embracing their True Identity as a Mime.

SOARING TO GOD'S PURPOSE

My journey into Eagle Nation has been an experience like nothing I have ever had before. I had always heard about the Eagles from those who ministered in dance but had never met one. I couldn't understand what the hype around the Eagles was, until I meet Prophetess Eagle Tanya Wormley at one of her prophetic conferences in 2017. She introduced me to the Eagles International Training Institute. Later that year, I registered for Dance Year One with Dr. Pamela as our instructor. I thought I knew about the ministry of dance, but after a few months in, I realized that I was taught wrong by other dance ministers.

One of our assignments/requirements was to come to a conference where Dr. Pamela was ministering and partake in the service. It was my first time meeting her. I was so excited about the conference, but I broke my toe right before the conference and came there with a boot on my foot. In our first session, we were in Dr. Pamela's class. I remember looking at her and thinking to myself, "This sweet little lady is powerful!" As she was teaching, she said something that still resonates with me to this day. Dr.

Pamela said, "You are a Masterpiece because you are a piece of the Master!" WOW!! Those words went straight to my heart, and from that moment, my life changed. I wanted to be an Eagle even more after those words.

At that same conference, the prophet spoke something to me that set me on fire! I forgot all about my foot, and I ran out of my boot around the huge conference room. My God, what have I experienced? I felt no pain, nothing! I came with only one shoe, so I was at the rest of the conference with that one shoe!

My first Summit was in 2018. Everything that could go wrong went wrong! I had to prepare for finals. I finished the written portion of the final, and I was overwhelmed. I did it! I graduated from Dance Year One! My family and friends all came to Texas to support me. Summit was an atmosphere of people from different nations coming together, not just to graduate but to praise God! I had never seen anything like this before! I was hooked.

I always knew that there was more to serving God but didn't know how or where to go to find it. Sometimes, you can feel stuck in your church because your zeal and passion don't match the environment of the church where you serve. I remember always going the extra mile in anything I did. I have always been a creative individual. I never wanted to keep the same hairstyles or look like everyone else. I knew I was different but didn't realize how different I was. I knew I was different from my sisters. As the oldest, I experienced life differently from them, especially after my mother passed. I was 14 years old. I didn't care about being different. I didn't care about what I did or about anyone's feelings. My sister and I had to move in with my father and his new family to a different state. I never grieved, I was rebellious, and I did everything under the sun, from selling crack cocaine to getting pregnant at the age of 16. My father was on drugs and abusive. My stepmother didn't care about us; she had a boyfriend and my father had a girlfriend. My sisters and I had to take care of ourselves. I didn't care about my own life or anyone else's, for that matter. However, due to a situation with a gun, I had to be removed from that state, and I couldn't come back until I was 21.

When God has a divine plan and purpose for your life, He will allow you to go through situations and persecution to appreciate where He has delivered you from. He will place you on the path that will direct you to Him. We just have to be obedient.

I was separated from my sisters and moved to Chicago, IL, with my aunt and uncle, a minister and an evangelist. Look at God. The setup was real. The Lord placed me into an environment, a home, where the Lord was worshipped and praised.

I thank God for my aunt and uncle giving me the foundation in my walk with the Lord. But I knew there was more to this walk. As I grew older and matured, I left the church that my aunt and uncle belonged to and attended a new church. I was captivated by the singing and teaching. It was different from the traditional church my aunt and uncle attended. My eyes and ears were open but not my heart.

I joined the new ministry, which I am still a member of today. End Times Full Gospel was a breath of fresh air. From here, I experienced praise and worship for the first time. Years later, I was one of the original members of the praise dance ministry. My journey had begun. For about ten years, I was under the impression that I thought I knew everything there was to know about praise dancing. Oh, the garments we wore!! LOL!! I can laugh about it now, but we were a hot mess. We used to get those scarves that said, "I Love Jesus," and get safety pins to make a top. Our garments were not garments; they were cheap material—dresses and shirts from Rainbow with a cross ironed on. Oh, we were so out of order!

Again, when God has a divine plan and purpose for your life, the environment will be provided for you. The people that He wants to teach and guide you will be in your path. It's about our yes to His will and His way.

As I said previously, I have always enjoyed arts and crafts. I started playing with fabric, and I asked one of my friends from the church who was older than me, Frenchy, who was a seamstress, to teach me how to sew. I was pregnant with my daughter and wasn't working at the time. I wanted to make our youth dance ministries a garment for the Christmas program. Frenchy was a wise seamstress. She was just a blessing to me on every level. She taught me everything I needed to know. She was so proud of me. So much so that she gave me my first sewing machine and serger. And as a badge of honor, she gave me her sewing box that I still have today. I started sewing by myself. Everything I made, I would show to her to get her opinion. The next thing I knew, she was having me teach her how to operate her new sewing and serger machines.

Once the Lord starts a fire in you, you have to keep adding wood to the flame. Keep the fire alive. I started making garments for our dance ministry, and the Lord just took my yes and elevated it to a different level. I knew there had to be more to this walk, more to learn, more to grow. What could I do to enhance my creativity for the Kingdom?

I started off with garments but didn't know that God set me up to create for the Kingdom of God. As I was preparing for graduation for Summit, I took it upon myself to make my own garments. I didn't want my garments to look like everyone else's, so I sat with the Holy Spirit, and He gave me a vision. From that vision, I created my dance final garment for Dance Year One. I made it the night before I left. The Holy Spirit instructed me to create it in red. I was obedient and created a beautiful garment in red. After I ministered my dance final, we had our first ministry meeting for the week of Summit. I was blown away at the dancing and singing. I had found my tribe. I had found a place where the people were like me, not ashamed to dance and sing before the Lord. Oh, I love everything about it. Then, the prophetic anointing started flowing. One of the prophets said, "Everyone who has on the color red, come to the front." Of course, I said to myself, "Lord, did you set me up?" But I went to the front as we were instructed. There were about 10 who had on red in a room full of people. This prophet, I believe his name was Bobby, was releasing God's word over people, and he came to me and said these words: "Your name will be known in the Kingdom Market Place. God will bestow upon your unique creations that no one will match. You will reach the nations with your hands."

Wow, straight to the floor ministry is where I went.

The Holy Spirit instructed me to create a garment in red because the Lord had a divine plan and purpose for me at my first EITI Summit. But He didn't stop there! I knew that Eagle Nation was a family of peculiar people who know that there is more to this walk in Christ. It was just a matter of opening my heart and receiving the directions from the Holy Spirit.

After graduation, I knew I wanted more, but what would be the next step? Worship! I remember that listening to Dr. Viven talking about God at Summit captivated me. I knew I had to take that class! I never thought that taking that course would direct me into who I am today!

I started making Kingdom Crowns. The more I studied worship, the more anointed my creativity became. I love it when someone tells me, "I saw one of your crowns in a ministry piece. I know it was one of yours because it looks like a Tammy Chambers Crown." Worship developed my creativity into a whole different level. Holy Spirit released me to create crowns, scepters, alabaster boxes, anointing oil bottles, and so much more. Worship changed my life. I love Dr. Vivien because the Lord used her to open my eyes to Him. My heart was now a temple for God's presence. I took Year One and Two of The School of Worship. After that, I graduated from Choregeo and released a book through the Authors Course. *Worship Because Your Life Depends On It* was birthed during that course.

Today, I am teaching School of Worship through The Eagle Network (TEN) and also teaching two School of Power and Activation (SOPAA) courses, "Worship Because Your Life Depends On It" and "Creating With Elohim," which Dr. Pamela specifically asked me to teach. She saw my passion for creativity for the Kingdom of God. I also serve as an admin for a couple of courses through the Eagles.

Joining the Eagles has soared me into my purpose in God. I never would have thought that I would serve as a teacher. It is a passion that I never knew I had. My journey is just beginning, and as I always end in all my Eagles emails, it is an honor to serve.

ABOUT THE AUTHOR

Minister Tammy Chambers is a worship theologian, owner of The Chambers Kingdom LLC, and leader of the Ministers of Movement. She has served as an altar worker at End Times Ministry for over 30 years and teaches worship courses for Eagles and SOPAA. She serves with her husband, Chris, and daughter, Chrishelle.

THE WEIGHT OF YES

I wasn't just helping because I wanted to. I was saying yes out of fear. Fear of rejection. Fear of being abandoned. Fear of not being enough. To the outside world, I was a giver. A helper. Someone who could always be counted on. If someone needed help, I was there. If an opportunity arose, I jumped in. If there was a way to serve, I made myself available. But behind every yes was a quiet desperation to be liked, to feel needed, to prove I mattered. And inside? I was exhausted. Overwhelmed. Carrying a deep, unmet need I didn't fully understand. My constant giving came at a cost: my health, my peace, and my most important relationships.

The turning point came when I fell to my knees and sought the Lord. He reminded me that my worth wasn't found in what I did for others but in who I was in Him. That's when I discovered the power of saying no, not as an act of selfishness, but as an act of obedience. Of wisdom. Of freedom.

Part 1: Recognizing the Root Cause

Before you can change, you must understand why you struggle with saying no. Many people-pleasers, like my old self, develop this pattern due to deep wounds. For me, it was rejection and abandonment. I wasn't saying yes just to be helpful; I was saying yes because I feared that if I didn't, I wouldn't be loved or accepted.

Rejection and abandonment stemmed from different places. My mother didn't know the identity of her biological father. She was also raised by the sister of her biological mother. This was always confusing for me as a child. Who do I call Grandma? Are you my cousin or my aunt? I didn't really know my biological father either. I only met him once or twice as a child.

Reflection Questions:

When do you feel the strongest urge to say yes?
Are you afraid that saying no will make others reject you?
Do you feel like your worth is tied to what you do for others?
Have you ever overcommitted to something and later regretted it?

These questions help uncover whether your yeses are truly coming from a place of love or from a place of fear.

Activation: Journaling Prayer

Find a quiet space and write a prayer to God, asking Him to reveal any wounds that drive your overcommitment. Ask Him to heal those areas and to help you see yourself through His eyes.

Getting to the root is the first step to freedom. Hallelujah! Now that the why behind the yes has been exposed, let's explore the cost.

Part 2: The Cost of Overcommitment

Saying yes to everything doesn't just drain your time; it drains your spirit. When you overextend yourself, you:

Damage your relationships because you're too busy for meaningful connection.

- My husband and I were like two ships that passed in the night. I always had meetings to go to, ministry functions to attend, school, work, rehearsals; you name it, I did it. I did everything but prioritize my marriage. My husband began resenting my extra activities, which led us to have countless arguments and seriously contemplate divorce.

Miss out on God's best because you're too distracted by trivial things.

- I accepted every invitation to minister in dance because I love it so much. Movement helps me purge negativity and enter into worship with the Lord. I was so flattered by the offer that most of the time I didn't pray first. When divine opportunities came up, I had to squeeze them in or turn them down. My stress levels were through the roof. And most importantly, I wasn't able to pour into the things God actually called me to do because I was too busy with things He never assigned to me. "Busy" became an idol.

Neglect your own health and well-being.

- Fast food, processed food, and Chinese takeout were my daily bread. As I went from one thing to the next, there was no time to cook or make healthy meals. A stop at the golden arches, Pizza Hut, or Popeye's chicken was always in order, or so I thought. I developed high blood pressure and cholesterol and exercised-induced asthma.

Experience chronic stress, which can lead to burnout and disease.

- At the age of 23, I was wearing a heart monitor. I experienced chest pains and palpitations regularly. I was everyone's counselor. No matter what their problem was, I searched for a solution. I wanted to fix everything. I wanted them to be happy and stress free. When I realized the burden of other people's problems was about to kill me, I immediately started stepping back. What I found out was that I had been hindering people from maturing and finding their own solutions. Some truly needed help; some just wanted to complain with no accountability; and some just wanted to be in my space. I needed boundaries.

Biblical Wisdom on Boundaries

- Jesus, our perfect example, did not say yes to everything. He often withdrew to pray (Luke 5:16) and did only what His Father instructed (John 5:19). If Jesus needed to set boundaries, so do we. We are not the savior.

Activation: Audit Your Commitments

- Take a piece of paper and write down everything you are currently committed to: ministries, work, friendships, family obligations, and any other responsibilities. Then, pray over this list, and ask God which ones are truly His assignments for you and which ones you need to release.

Now that you've finished your audit, it's time to take your power back. Are you ready to be obedient and let go?

Part 3: Learning to Say No (Without Guilt)

When I first tried saying no, I wrestled with guilt like it was a spiritual test I was failing. I believed I was letting people down, missing divine assignments, or being un-Christlike. But the truth is, Jesus didn't say yes to everything. He didn't heal every sick person in Israel. He didn't answer every demand. He walked away from the crowds to be alone with the Father.

Saying no doesn't mean you're selfish. It means you're surrendered. You're choosing alignment with God's will over applause from people.

Once I realized that saying yes to everything was not godly, I had to learn how to say no. At first, it felt foreign and uncomfortable. But the more I did it, the freer I felt. I got good at it. My team says I can say no so eloquently now that they can't even get mad.

Biblical Affirmations for Saying No

"Let your yes be YES. Let your no be NO" (Matthew 5:37 NLV).

"Am I now trying to win the approval of human beings, or of God?" (Galatians 1:10 NIV).

"God is not a God of disorder but of peace" (1 Corinthians 14:33 NIV).

Practical Ways to Say No Gracefully

Be Direct, But Kind – "I appreciate the opportunity, but I won't be able to commit."

Offer an Alternative – "I can't help this time, but I can suggest someone else."

Set Boundaries – "I have to prioritize my health/family/time with God, so I need to decline."

Use Scripture – "I'm seeking the Lord about my commitments, and I don't feel called to this right now."

The Power of a Spirit-Led No

When you say no from a place of obedience, it:

Protects your purpose.

Cultivates inner peace.

Honors your body and mind.

Reflects your trust in God as your Source.

Saying yes to every opportunity may actually be disobedience if God didn't assign it. And that disobedience, even when well-intentioned, can delay your destiny.

Scriptural Support for Boundaries and Priorities

"Above all else, guard your heart, for everything you do flows from it" (Proverbs 4:23 NIV).

"For everything there is a season, a time for every activity under heaven" (Ecclesiastes 3:1 NLT).

In Mark 1:35-38, Jesus left the crowd and chose to move on, even when more people wanted healing. He stayed focused on His assignment.

Types of No You Need in Your Vocabulary

1. The Protective No – "No, I can't take this on because it conflicts with what God is asking of me right now."
2. The Peace-Preserving No – "No, I'm at capacity and need to honor my limits."
3. The Strategic No – "No, I'm focusing on my core assignments in this season."
4. The Compassionate No – "I love you and want the best for you, but I can't be the one to help this time."

Activation: Boundaries Map

Draw a circle on a blank sheet of paper. Inside, list your top God-given priorities (e.g., family, health, ministry, your calling). Outside the circle, write everything that is distracting or draining you. These are your potential no's. Start praying through how to release or reassign those obligations.

Practice saying no in the mirror. Remember to smile.

Was that so bad? It's okay if the answer is yes. Soon it will feel more natural. Now, let's see how the power of your no will realign you with your destiny.

Part 4: Clearing Your Plate With God's Guidance

As I stepped into a season of surrender, I asked God to show me what truly mattered. He led me to lay some things down and focus on the assignments He had actually given me. What does that look like? I disassociated with some ministry groups and organizations. I retired from the military. I resigned from a very profitable MLM. I released some friends that were draining.

I started to pray about everything for real. And, most importantly, to wait for an answer. I don't want to move unless led by Holy Spirit. I understand now that God is with me always, so why not get advice from the Creator Himself? That is a true privilege.

Steps to Clear Your Plate:

Pray for Discernment – Ask God which commitments to keep and which to let go.

List Your Priorities – Align your commitments with God's will, your purpose, and your health.

Start Letting Go – Begin stepping back from obligations that are not meant for you.

Guard Your Time – Set boundaries to prevent future overcommitment.

Activation: The "God's Will" Filter

Before saying yes to anything, ask yourself:

Does this align with God's purpose for my life?

Will this bring peace or stress?

Am I saying yes out of love or fear?

Will this take me away from my God-given priorities?

If the answer to any of these is not what you would hope for, it's okay to say no. It's time to get free, stay free, and set other people free!

Part 5: Living in Freedom

Freedom is more than just rest. It's knowing you're in alignment with Heaven. As I started saying no, I began to feel lighter. My time opened up. My stress decreased. My creativity returned. And most of all, I felt God's pleasure, not because I was doing more, but because I was doing what He asked.

What Freedom Looks Like in Real Life

You stop apologizing for needing rest.

You decline invitations without guilt.

You steward your energy and protect your anointing.

You embrace margin, time to think, pray, dream, and enjoy your life.

You trust that God will meet the needs of others without you being the savior.

God didn't create you to be everyone's answer. He created you to be a vessel, not a vending machine. When you stop rushing and striving, you start thriving.

Scriptural Foundation for Freedom and Peace

> "I came that they may have and enjoy life, and have it in abundance [to the full, till it overflows]" (John 10:10 AMP).

> "For all who have entered into God's rest have rested from their labors ..." (Hebrews 4:10 NLT).

> "You keep him in perfect peace whose mind is stayed on you, because he trusts in you" (Isaiah 26:3 ESV).

Strategies for Living in Freedom With Boundaries

1. Daily Check-Ins With God – Start each day with this prayer: "Lord, order my steps. Block what's not for me."

2. Sabbath Rhythm – Practice rest weekly. Your value doesn't decrease when you pause.
3. Build a No-Team – Surround yourself with people who support your boundaries and will help you enforce them.

Now that I've learned the power of saying no, I walk in more peace, joy, and purpose. I no longer feel guilty for turning down things that aren't aligned with God's plan. I have more time for my family, my health, and the assignments God has truly given me.

I want the same for you. God has not called you to live in constant stress and burnout. He wants you to live in the fullness of His peace.

Activation: Declarations of Freedom

Speak these aloud over yourself:

I am not obligated to every opportunity; I am called to obedience.

Saying no is a holy boundary.

I do not need to be needed to be valuable.

I am led by peace, not pressure.

My "no" creates space for God's best "yes."

Final Activation: Prayer of Release

Pray this out loud:

"Lord, I surrender my need for approval. I release every commitment that is not from You. I trust that my worth is not in what I do but in who I am in You. Give me wisdom to say yes to the right things and the strength to say no to everything else. Fill me with Your peace, and help me walk in obedience. In Jesus' name, Amen."

Your No Is Powerful

Saying no is not selfish. It is obedience. When you clear your plate, you make room for God's best. You are not here to please people; you are here to serve the Lord.

If you struggle with people-pleasing, I encourage you to start today. Take small steps. Pray. Set boundaries. Trust that God will honor your obedience. And remember, your yes is valuable, so don't give it away lightly.

Let's walk in freedom together.

ABOUT THE AUTHOR

S. Dee Clark-Riley is an award-winning author, international speaker, and founder of Kingdom Worshippers International and We Are All Sons. A retired member of the Air Force Chaplain Corp, she now empowers others through Christian coaching, worship arts, and holistic wellness. Connect with this powerhouse @ dee3271@gmail.com, or visit www.sdeeclarkriley.com.

FROM SCARCITY TO ABUNDANCE: MY JOURNEY TO SUCCESS AND FINANCIAL FREEDOM

Apostle Ingrid Conliffe-Easton was born in Guyana and lived in Aruba. She is an experienced financial strategist dedicated to promoting debt-free living. With over 20 years in the industry, she specializes in debt management, budgeting, and legacy building. Her meticulous approach and critical thinking help clients live financially empowered lives.

Every individual possesses a unique story, one that shows their struggles, resilience, and eventual success. My path from hardship to financial independence showcases the battles fought and lessons learned as well as the unwavering determination and faith that have propelled me forward.

In the wild skies, eagles embody the spirit of transformation. When bound by scarcity, they rise above limitations, symbolizing resilience and strength. Each morning, an eagle awakens with a hunger for more than survival; they crave the thrill of soaring high, scouting the vast expanse for opportunities.

A Childhood Shaped by Determination

My journey mirrors my own struggle with debt and the pursuit of being debt free. Just as eagles learn to harness the wind, I learned to master my finances while navigating my current situation. With a flap of their powerful wings, eagles break free from the weight of their past, embarking on a path toward abundance and whatever they set their sights on. Through determination and vision, they conquer the skies. This reminded me that debt does not define me. So, I embraced the spirit of perseverance that led me to a brighter horizon, where financial successes became not just a destination but a way of life.

Life can often feel like climbing a big mountain. My journey from just getting by to being financially free has been a journey of intentionality. I have faced many challenges, including norms, fear, and doubt. Nevertheless, the journey from just enough to achieving financial freedom has been a fulfillment of what I heard the Lord say to me as a teenager at the altar in a youth camp. Through faith, resilience, and unwavering support from my beloved husband, I transformed our lives by being strong and tenacious. *"I can do all things through Christ who strengthens me"* (Philippians 4:13 NKJV). This does not only apply to me; it shows that we collectively can overcome tough times and that success is possible for everyone.

I grew up in a single-parent household with my mom, brother, and sister. During my early childhood, my mom worked as a maid and did her best to make sure we were well taken care of. I knew growing up that life was not necessarily easy, but being the last of three kids had its advantages. I was spoiled by my mom, who tried very hard to give me everything I wanted.

My mom was ambitious in her own way. She learned about a program that would allow folks to attend a series of meetings to learn about homeownership. From the very beginning, everyone in the program was told there were no guarantees as to who would be chosen to receive a house. However, this did not deter my mom. Every Friday evening, we would walk back and forth for miles to attend these meetings. As God would have it, my mom was chosen to receive a house.

Everyone chosen worked tirelessly as a community to build these houses. The work was supervised by professionals, and no one knew which house was going to be theirs. After months of working together, the project was completed, and each individual was given a house. My mom took great pride in being a homeowner. Her tenacity and drive left an indelible mark on my life.

Throughout high school and college, I found education relatively easy and rarely studied. Case in point, in Bible College, I borrowed my roommate's notes the night before an exam. She had been studying for a few weeks, and I asked to look at her notes the night before the exam. When the grades were posted, she scored 97, and I received 95, causing her to berate me. She was very upset because I got almost the same grade without studying as she did.

The Call to Ministry and the Cost of Obedience

After graduating from high school, I found employment at a private school, where most of the students were children of government officials. Before this time, my sister was the only breadwinner. So she was very happy when I got the opportunity to interview for a teaching position at a high school. There was no doubt that I would have gotten the job. However, a few months prior, I had started having internal battles with the call of God on my life. The struggles deepened, and on the day of the interview, I decided not to go; that meant I had made the decision to attend Bible School. I was acutely aware of the problems this decision would cause at home. Needless to say, my sister was furious when she learned I had not gone for the interview. I recall her crying profusely and saying I was selfish and unfair.

During this time, I found solace in the fact that I knew without a shadow of a doubt that I was supposed to attend Bible School because I was called to the ministry. *"Be of good courage, and he shall strengthen your heart, all ye that hope in the Lord"* (Psalm 31:24 KJV). This is a reminder that we must remain steadfast in our pursuits.

It was in Bible School that I met my wonderful husband of almost 45 years, while he was attending his nephew's wedding in Guyana. Two years after that, I migrated to Aruba, and we got married. We are blessed with three children and a granddaughter.

Prior to my arriving in Aruba, my intended husband rented a three-bedroom, two-bathroom house. So, after staying with friends in order to satisfy the Dutch law of being on the island three months before marriage, I was able to move into my own home after our wedding.

My life in Aruba was very challenging for months in the beginning within the church world. Although I was in the midst of people I knew from Bible School in Guyana, I was made to feel like an outsider, memories and instances of which I will not divulge here. Suffice it to say, the old adage is true: "Come see me and come live with me are two different things." Nevertheless, I was involved in church work—namely, the worship team, youth group, Sunday school, and Bible School over the years.

A Shocking Phone Call and a Financial Wake-Up

In spite of everything I went through, my husband was my rock, source of comfort, and strength. So one day, when I was sitting at the kitchen table, the phone rang, and the conversation really rocked my world. My sister asked how much money I had in the bank. It was a mere fifty-two dollars.

The reason was that I was a stay-at-home mom with my husband being the sole provider. He had decided a few years earlier that because of the call of God on my life for ministry, I was not going into the workforce. As he phrased it, he did not want to get in "trouble with God." But as my sister spoke, I knew I needed to make a change. The time spent always navigating our finances and realizing we did not have enough money to meet our commitments frightened me all over again.

Thoughts of not being good enough plagued my mind. If an emergency happened, according to statistics, I would struggle because like 56% of the population, I could not afford an emergency bill of a thousand dollars (cnbc.com).

Reality told me I needed to learn how to master money because I was just spending the little I had without accountability to myself or anyone else. I realized I was fighting against the stigma of living from paycheck to paycheck.

When Faith Meets Finance

One day, I was told about a position as an advertising agent for a chain of restaurants. I interviewed for the position and was hired immediately. I flourished in this position, and the restaurant grew from one to three restaurants with different cuisines. After being there for over a year, I was recruited by one of the time-share resorts on the island. I remained in this industry for the next 15-plus years, where I was a top producer in both the marketing and sales departments.

Money was no longer a problem. Now I was on the other side of the spectrum, spending money wildly again with no accountability. We were going to Disney with the kids with spending money that could have been a down payment on a property. So now we were acting foolishly. However, remember, you don't know what you don't know. The one good thing in this situation was the fact that I was an avid saver also.

What became life-changing for us was when we decided to embark on a debt-free lifestyle. Unlike some of my friends, who were changing cars every year and squandering their money, we were committed to making a change.

Later on, as a family, we migrated to America. It was through being here and really understanding financial literacy and the opportunities here that we excelled as a family. I began to view my beginning struggles as stepping stones rather than obstacles.

Education, Elevation, and Europe!

As my children prepared to enter college, the thought came to mind, why not go to college? I had been out of a traditional school setting for over 30 years. Very soon, the thought took root, and I entered college with my kids. I was fortunate enough to attend both Georgia Perimeter College and then Georgia State University on a free ride. Again, the Lord worked mysteriously for me and opened doors that no man can shut (Revelation 3:8).

In college, I was the vice president of the Phi Beta Kappa, and at university, I was a McNair Scholar—a program I got into without being a STEM student. As a McNair Scholar, I had the opportunity to attend the University of Salamanca in Spain. I was also the vice-president of the hospitality student association. Again, this was not my major, but God! This position gave me the opportunity and privilege of visiting seven countries in Europe. All these opportunities and skills learned proved to be invaluable, and I excelled, not only for myself but for those who believed in me. This positive outlook made it easier to tackle challenges head-on, allowing me to focus on solutions rather than problems and to experience success.

I presently hold an associate degree, three bachelor's degrees (presently pursuing a master's for January '26 graduation), a real estate license, and insurance licenses in four states, along with other diplomas and certifications. God has really been good to me, and I rejoice in His goodness and faithfulness. *"'For I know the plans I have for you,' declares the Lord, 'plans to prosper you and not to harm you, plans to give you hope and a future'"* (Jeremiah 29:11 NIV).

This eagle has been soaring all because of the grace of God. I have traveled to over 38 countries and counting, several of which I have visited more than once. To God be the glory!

My first job after graduating from university was as a real estate agent. I was fortunate to help a young man buy several houses. I worked hard: *"And whatsoever ye do, do it heartily, as to the Lord, and not unto men"* (Colossians 3:23 KJV).

As time passed, I joined LegalShield and became a presenter for my local group. My hard work paid off with promotions and more responsibilities. When challenges came up, I remembered my past struggles, which kept me focused. I learned to manage my money and avoid unnecessary spending. I followed the advice of Proverbs 21:20(NIV): *"The wise store up choice food and olive oil, but fools gulp theirs down."* I was on my way to an exciting and stable future.

Legacy First, Then Luxury!

Now, I am known as a wealth and legacy architech. I love my job, which includes owning real estate and helping clients manage their finances. I am thankful for my journey. *"They that wait upon the Lord shall renew their strength; they shall mount up with wings as eagles; they shall run and not grow weary; they shall walk and not be faint"* (Isaiah 40:31 KJV).

Throughout all my many challenges, I have learned important lessons. I learned that if you don't give up and have faith, dreams can become reality. Challenges become opportunities to learn and grow. In hard times, I found strength through my faith, my beliefs, and the Bible. I believe that as I share my story, others will be encouraged. My motto is, "If I can do this, so can you." Anyone can rise above the fray and difficulties with hard work, faith, and determination.

To all reading this, never lose hope. Change is possible! Here are some simple steps on how you can get started:

1. Break your goals into smaller steps, and don't give up, no matter how slow progress seems.
2. Look for knowledge and support from others. Surround yourself with positive people, and ignore the naysayers.
3. Reflect on your journey; each challenge prepares you for future successes.

Remember Philippians 3:14 (KJV): *"I press toward the mark for the prize of the high calling of God in Christ Jesus."* You have limitless potential! Each step you take brings you closer to success.

Reflecting, I see the value in every struggle and success I experienced. My story shows that hard work and determination can unleash your potential. I trust that my experiences will inspire each reader. Regardless of where you started, you can overcome obstacles and achieve your dreams.

The Wisdom of an Eagle!

Remember these truths about eagles:

1. They have clear vision.
2. They fly high, often alone.
3. They are brave and never give up.
4. They are persistent.
5. They don't eat dead things (gossiping).
6. They prepare for new challenges.
7. They are full of energy.

You can have these same qualities too, with Jesus being your Helper. I believe in you; go forth and conquer in Jesus' mighty name, Amen. Blessings!

"I declare that scarcity ends with me, and abundance flows through me. I am the head and not the tail. I lend and do not borrow. My hands build legacy and my heart beats with Kingdom purpose." Hallelujah!

Phone #: 404-543-2819

Email: ingridconliffe@gmail.com / ice.moneymatters@gmail.com

ABOUT THE AUTHOR

Apostle Ingrid Conliffe-Easton was born in Guyana and lived in Aruba. She is an experienced financial strategist dedicated to promoting debt-free living. With over 20 years in the industry, she specializes in debt management, budgeting, and legacy building. Her meticulous approach and critical thinking help clients live financially empowered lives.

THE POWER OF WAITING!

Chapter Dedication

This chapter is dedicated to Dr. Pamela Scott. Thank you for activating me into fulfilling God's purpose for my life. I am grateful for your anointing, your leadership, your sacrifice, and your love for Kingdom advancement. I also dedicate this chapter to Eagle Nation. We SOAR together.

Introduction – The Storm Before the Storm

On February 7, 2023, my husband of almost 30 years, the Reverend Rodney E. Dailey, was called home to be with the Lord after a courageous fight with cancer. I could never imagine life without Rodney, although Rodney would always think of me, saying, "I need you to know how to do this, just in case I am not here one day."

The reality of the "one day" did not seem possible until the "one day" became the one day.

Five years before his death, we received his stage four cancer diagnosis; the cancer had metastasized. During these five years, God took us on a journey that only strengthened our faith and marriage. Yes, we went and got a second doctor's opinion and ultimately decided to move forward with treatment. Continuous doctors' appointments, medications, treatments, and the impacts of those became part of our routine.

I had a full-time job, was pastoring a church, was teaching, and was now taking care of Rodney in a new way. At first, it seemed like I could manage, but as Rodney grew sicker, my capacity began to shrink as I needed to focus more on taking care of my husband. At first, I was trying to do it all, but I slowly realized, with the help of Holy Spirit, that I had to slow things down. I could not do it all at the same pace and same level as before.

I really had to tell myself that it was okay to slow things down. As an overachiever and an Eagle that SOARS, it was hard for me to slow things down. But the more Rodney's health began to deteriorate, the more God continued to reveal to me why and how I needed to slow it down.

The Storm

The storm was happening; I was right in the middle of it and had to learn how to SOAR differently. I was soaring alright, navigating, adjusting, and going to new heights. But what the Lord revealed to me was that I had a new perspective on soaring. This was not about the kingdom advancement or ministry assignments or successful engagements I had been used to. This was a new type of kingdom advancement, a new ministry assignment, and a successful engagement that the Lord assigned me to, and in that assignment, the Lord shifted my capacity and ability to care for my husband in a new way in the last season of his life. I was SOARING to new heights in my spiritual development, new heights in my faith, and new heights in my relationship with the Lord! I had to trust at new levels, seek His guidance and strength at higher levels. I had to go to the highest mountain in order to complete the assignment I had that season, and that was to take care of my husband, who was in hospice care at home because he wanted to be at home and I was able to do it. I was SOARING to new heights, through the pain, uncertainty, and exhaustion. I was SOARING!

The definition of "soar" according to Merriam -Webster is:

- to fly aloft or about
- to hover in the air often at a great height
- to rise or increase dramatically (as in position, value, or price)
- to ascend to a higher or more exalted level

So often, we can equate SOARING with external factors that are often measured by external indicators. But what God revealed to me was that in this season of pain and uncertainty and sacrifice, I had to adjust to the readjustment of my flight plan, which took me to the highest mountain to stay there for a while. Although I had to pause, I was not taken off God's list for His plan for my life.

You may be going through a season of taking care of a loved one who cannot take care of themselves: a parent, spouse, child, or relative. Know that God will give you everything you need to complete the assignment. You may feel like you can't do this or you don't have the strength or the stamina, but trust that God will see you through. Remember this: *"Casting all your anxieties on him, because he cares for you"* (1 Peter 5:7 ESV).

My New Drumbeat!

After Rodney's passing, I had to learn how to live life to a different drumbeat. My rhythm in life had to change. How I operated and functioned in the world had to change. Was I ready for it? No. Was I able to do it? Yes!

I must say that my Eagle Family showed up. Not only did they pray for me and call me, but Eagles also came to my husband's homegoing service. My Apostle, my spiritual mother, Pamela Scott, came herself to offer support. This blessed my soul and encouraged and strengthened me. I was part of an international family that had a wingspan of over 22 nations and three continents. The prayers and condolences truly were from across the globe.

Eagle Nation helped me weather the storm. Eagle Nation picked up my wings when they were broken. Eagle Nation prayed me into healing, comfort, and strength.

How was I able to adjust, readjust, shift, and flow? I had to continue to WAIT. In the midst of it all—the storm, the pain, the grief—I had to continue life without my partner, my friend, my lover, with a life that was now different.

A Time to Wait!

My life did not go back to the way it was. I was still on the mountain. Just waiting on the Lord. I tried to go back to life the way it was—my activities, ministry, work—but I couldn't. I had to wait.

> "But they that wait upon the Lord shall renew their strength; they shall mount up with wings as eagles; they shall run, and not be weary; and they shall walk, and not faint." (Isaiah 40:31 KJV).

The Hebrew word for wait is *qāvâ*, and it means to wait, look for, hope, expect. God shut everything down for a season. All of the extra things I could not take on. I had to clear my plate, allow myself to grieve, and wait. Waiting strengthened my faith; I had to go deeper in my relationship with the Lord. I spent more time in prayer, reading His word, fasting, and reflecting. I was in a season of waiting. I did not have the energy or the mental capacity to do anything above and beyond the basics. I had to allow myself to grieve and to have the space to deal with all the other things that go along with grief, and it was okay. It was necessary. It was healing, and it set me up for the next move of God in my life. But I had to wait. Yes, the world kept moving. Yes, there were things I had to say no to, but it was the best for me and my family, who also needed me during this season of grief.

A Renewed Strength!

My testimony is that they that wait shall renew their strength. I have finally been released from the Lord from my season of waiting, and Oh Boy! I have a renewed strength. Because I waited on the Lord, I have renewed my strength. I have clarity, vision, revelation, and insight, which have propelled me to new heights.

I want to remind you that your waiting is not in vain. You may be at the beginning, in the middle, or near the end. Just wait. God will give you what you need when you need it. Your breakthrough is coming. Your season for waiting will come to an end. Wait on the Lord because after your wait, God will give you a renewed strength that will position you to SOAR even higher than before.

It will be time to mount up. Because I waited, because you waited, we are mounting up. We shall mount up with wings like an eagle.

To mount up means to go up, to ascend, to come up (of animals), to spring up, to grow, to shoot forth (of vegetation). To go up over, rise (of natural phenomenon), to come up (before God), to excel, to gain momentum, to gain strength.

The wait is over. It is time to mount up to new heights, new destinations, new assignments, new relationships, new resources, new revelations, new insights, and a new level in our relationship with God. This is my story. My life has changed. I'm still alive, and although I could not have imagined my life this way, I have trusted in the Lord with all my heart, and He has certainly directed my path.

I am an Eagle, soaring to new heights and new places. I waited, and it blessed my soul. *"Wait for the Lord; be strong and take heart and wait for the Lord"* (Psalm 27:14 NIV).

Call to Action

Soaring continues even through pain. I just had to SOAR to new heights, realizing my purpose was not placed on pause but that the pause was part of my purpose. It was only in my waiting that I caught the revelation.

When you wait on the Lord, you will not stray from His plan for your life. Remember, He is just preparing you to go higher.

Mount up, and get ready for the highest mountain.

ABOUT THE AUTHOR

Janine Dailey has a unique calling to activate believers and to help deliver them from religious strongholds. She is the founder of New Wine Ministries, an apostolic training hub to activate, equip, and send believers to fulfill their kingdom assignment. She is also a faculty member at the Eagles International Training Institute, where she trains and equips leaders and ministers from all over the world. Additionally, she is an ordained itinerant elder in the African Methodist Episcopal Church (AMEC)and currently serves as a pastor in the AMEC.

HIS ROYAL DIADEM

The Wilderness

The night was thick with silence, except for the whisper of my own breath. A once-familiar world had been stripped from me, leaving only the echoes of footsteps walking away. Twenty-five years of love, labor, and sacrifice, gone with the turning of a calendar page. I was no longer a wife. No longer a woman whose world revolved around the laughter of her children in the next room. I was alone.

But not abandoned.

Though the weight of heartbreak pressed against my chest, something deeper stirred within me. A whisper. A calling. A gentle, unrelenting pull toward the throne of the King who had never forsaken me. On New Year's Day, I fell to my knees, tears soaking the floor as I dialed into the prophetic intercession community, Thy Kingdom Come prayer line, for the first time. What began as a desperate search for solace became a consuming hunger for the presence of God. One hour turned into two. Then three. Then seven. Then ten. The more I poured out, the more He poured in.

I was still standing. No, I was rising.

The Awakening

Through the storm, I encountered faces draped in both kindness and deceit. Some came with empty hands and full hearts; others came with full hands and empty souls. I saw it all. The way a heart wears its truth, broadcasting its flaws like an untuned radio. As a seer, I'd always been able to perceive the hidden wounds in others, yet I'd misjudged who was meant to walk beside me. Some were never meant to be close, only assignments. And in my longing for intimacy, I'd let them too near.

Familiarity had bred contempt. Trust had been misplaced. Love had been misused.

For years, I built up walls around my heart to shield myself from recurring disappointments, unmet emotional needs, and a slow erosion of trust and identity. There were times when I felt unseen, unheard, and unsupported in the very place that should have been my sanctuary. I gave and gave, trying to keep everything together— the home, the family, the faith, the dreams—until I had nothing left to hold onto.

There were betrayals, broken promises, and many unspoken wounds that silently bled beneath the surface. And yet, for years, I stayed silent. I rationalized. I prayed. I endured. Because I believed in the covenant I'd made and the family we had built.

But then came the day when the silence became unbearable, when the weight of pretending threatened to suffocate my soul.

And in that sacred moment, I chose me. I chose healing. I chose peace. I chose to believe that God had more for me than cycles of sorrow. On July 4, 2023, I filed for divorce. A declaration of independence, not just legally but also spiritually.

Leaving was not easy. I left with nothing but my faith—no savings, no safety net. I had to move over an hour away from my children, which broke me in places I didn't know could fracture. I am a mother through and through, the kind who hosts family dinners, game nights, birthday parties, and school pickups. Being apart from my children felt like having my heart stretched across a thousand miles. I grieved as though someone had died.

Still, I prayed. Still, I believed.

The Rebuilding

I moved into a single room in my Eagle Mother's home. I was 19 when I married; now, here I was, starting over, alone in a world I didn't recognize. I became quiet. Withdrawn. I tried to take up as little space as possible, not wanting to disturb anyone with my sorrow. Outwardly, I smiled, but inside, I was wrestling with depression, anxiety, and crippling fear.

I felt invisible. Overlooked. Displaced. Like no one around me truly understood the depth of what I was facing. My unhealed wounds manifested as crippling sciatica, making each step painfully difficult and requiring the healing touch of a chiropractor.

And still, I prayed. Still, I believed.

In February 2024, things began to shift. With the financial help of my mother and friend, I rented a three-bedroom townhome. In May, when school let out, my youngest son came to live with me full-time, and my other children visited. I was overjoyed. But just as quickly, another wave came crashing. A real-estate deal I was working on fell through at the closing table. A major client canceled a contract in the same month. Suddenly, I couldn't pay my rent for August.

I worked out a payment arrangement with my landlord—three payments split between September, October, and November. Then, I met a beautiful woman at church who helped me walk into a job in three days without even applying. I thought, *this is God!* But before I could finish the payment plan, the job let me go, citing that I wasn't a good fit.

Back in a financial bind, I communicated with the landlord, hoping to continue working things out. But once he realized the unit could be quickly rented, he moved forward with eviction. When the eviction was rendered, I filed an appeal to buy more time to pay the arrears.

Women lifted me in prayer, their intercession like incense rising to heaven. Two from my church life group opened their hearts and hands, sowing into my storm with quiet strength. When I shared my truth online, raw and real, my NJ and Eagles sister responded with love that felt like the flood of heaven breaking through.

I thought, *surely the Lord is moving. This wave of grace is the prelude to my miracle.*

I filed my taxes, faith anchoring every keystroke, believing the provision would rush in like a flood to wipe the debt clean.

But it didn't.

However, in the midst, God had sent something deeper—one sister-friend, radiant and resolute.

A pillar of love.

Wise. Steady. Safe.

She walked with me through every twist, not as a visitor to my pain, but as a treasure given from a covenant-keeping God.

When we went to court the second time, the ruling came down. I was evicted and given five days to move.

With internal tears and faith in my bones, I packed my things. Again.

Even when I questioned my worth, even when people spoke to me with dishonor, even when circumstances screamed that I was forgotten, God still calls me Queen. He calls me worthy. He calls me His.

He whispers it in the midnight hour. He confirms it in His Word. I am not forsaken. I am not rejected. I am His Royal Diadem, set apart and adorned as a bejeweled crown fashioned by His hands.

The Coronation

I've known for a long time that the Lord created me for world-changing impact, even when my life didn't reflect the grandeur that burned within. When everything around me—the voices, the patterns—told me to trust nothing I saw and heard, I carried a knowing, a divine revelation.

I've never looked or sounded like the ones the church culture deemed worthy. I wasn't polished or perfect. I wasn't "churchy" enough. I grew up in church, but religion never stuck. I learned early on to be seen and not heard, so it was easy for me to shrink to protect myself. I silenced myself. I doubted my worthiness. I disqualified my voice so that others didn't have to. It's saddening how often I retreated to old patterns of bondage in search of safety.

At thirteen, I sought the Lord on my own. I joined the youth choir and signed myself up for youth retreats. It was at my first retreat that I experienced something Holy. I wanted to "shout," to dance before the Lord like I'd seen others do. So I prayed—simply, sincerely. The next morning during worship, I was overtaken. My body moved in praise, not by my own effort but by His Spirit. It was like an out-of-body experience, pure joy, pure beauty, pure presence.

That moment was the beginning. It was confirmation: He hears me and RESPONDS!

As I matured, I studied. I took classes and courses. I read books. I led ministries. I taught. I coached. I poured into women. Yet, those closest to me didn't honor the weight of what I carried. Their lack of acknowledgment had me questioning my authority, so I again began to retreat from my voice.

But God, in His faithfulness, always restored me. At my lowest, He would send a word, a prophetic confirmation, that reminded me of who I am and what He promised. These words became my anchors. I captured them, reread them, and held them close. They became my reminders in the dark: His Word will come to pass.

So I wept, but I worshipped. I was broken, but I burned for Him. And in my seeking, He led me to my tribe, Sisters Uknighted, a sisterhood woven by intercession, laughter, and unshakable faith. Though we are scattered across the map, we are bound in spirit. We lift each other, pray each other whole, and hold each other up when the weight of life presses down.

The seasons turned, and with each dawn, the ashes of my past were traded for something greater. I've walked through fire and emerged refined. My faith had been stretched, my identity reformed. The woman who once doubted her own radiance now stood among queens, clothed in grace, moving in purpose.

I'd lost what the world deemed everything but gained what was truly priceless.

Elevation had come, not by my striving but by His hand. He positioned me before mentors who spoke truth and wisdom into my destiny. He surrounded me with those rich in both character and resources. Where there had been lack, there is now overflow. Where there had been sorrow, there is now joy indescribable.

So, just like the woman with the alabaster jar, I bring my offering. My life, my worship, my everything. I pour my fragrant oil upon the feet of my King, for He alone is worthy.

I stand, His Royal Diadem, crowned not by circumstance but by His unwavering love.

And now, beloved, what about you? Perhaps you, too, know the weight of heavy sorrow, the stings and stabs of betrayal, the uncertainty of what lies ahead. I invite you to step into the presence of the One who never abandons. Build your fortress of intimacy through worship and prayer. Establish your secret place where the deafening volume of the world fades, and only His voice remains.

The journey is not easy, but YOU ARE WORTH IT. You were created with divine purpose, intricately designed by the hands of the Almighty. No storm can steal what He has spoken over your life. No betrayal can diminish the calling He has placed upon you. You are not forgotten. You are not forsaken. YOU ARE HIS.

Rise, daughter of the King. Take your place. Walk boldly in the favor and anointing He has released over you. When the world tells you that you are broken, remind yourself that He makes all things new. When circumstances scream you are unworthy, declare that you are chosen, beloved, and adorned with His favor.

Let this be the moment you shift. Let this be the moment you vow your love to the One who has never left you.

And when the trials come, when the fire burns and the wind blows, remember: You Are His Royal Diadem. And You Will Rise.

— Queen Chi

Now that you've walked with me through the fire, let me show you how to rise from its ashes. I've learned that even in the deepest moments of devastation, there is a calling to rebuild, reclaim, and reignite what is most precious within. The same steps that carried me through the storm can carry you through yours. Let us step forward together into the promise of new beginnings.

Practical Empowerment

Build Your Fortress of Intimacy and Purpose

1. Establish Your Secret Place

    Choose a consistent place in your home, small and simple, and make it your altar. This is where you meet with God. Add whatever draws your spirit into stillness and connection. Show up daily. He will meet you.

2. Cultivate a Rhythm of Intimacy

    Start with what you have—ten minutes or more. Some days will be full of worship, others quiet and still. All of it is worship. Be consistent. Be real.

3. Journal What You Hear and See

    Write down prayers, dreams, prophetic words, and divine impressions. These become anchors in your faith journey. Rehearse what God has spoken over you. Recite the scriptures. Revisit the dreams. Trust His promises; His Word won't fail.

4. Declare Truth Over Your Life

Each morning, I declare truth from scripture:

- Job 22:28 & Matthew 18:18 – My words establish God's purposes.
- Ephesians 2:6 – I rule from a heavenly seat.
- 1 Corinthians 15:57 & Deuteronomy 3:8 – I fight from victory.
- Romans 15:13 & 1 Peter 1:8 – I live in peace and joy.
- Matthew 5:14 & Isaiah 60:1-3 – I shine with His glory.

- Isaiah 22:22 – I access divine doors and favor.
- Proverbs 13:22 & Genesis 12:2 – I steward wealth and increase.

5. Surround Yourself with Faith-Filled Community

Find those who will pray with you, speak life, and help you stand. A godly sisterhood is a lifeline.

Scriptures That Anchor Me:

- Isaiah 62:3 – You are a crown of glory, a royal diadem in His hand.
- Jeremiah 29:11 – His plans for you are good.
- Psalm 34:18 – He is close to the brokenhearted.
- Romans 8:28 – All things work together for your good.

These steps may seem small, but they carry power. The same God who met me in the wilderness will meet you right where you are. He has not forgotten you. He is forming you.

Closing Prayer

Abba Father, Thank You for every heart that has journeyed through these words. Thank You for the hidden places where You've met us—in the pain, in the silence, in the questioning. Thank You that not one tear has been wasted, and not one moment of suffering is beyond Your redemption.

I lift up Your daughter now, the one who is reading with trembling hands or tear-filled eyes. Wrap her in Your presence. Let Your peace silence the noise of fear and doubt. Remind her that she is not forgotten, not forsaken, and never alone.

Breathe fresh wind into her weary soul. Restore her joy. Revive her purpose. Reignite her confidence. Anoint her eyes to see herself the way You do—crowned, chosen, radiant, and royal.

Give her strength to build her own secret place with You, where your power and presence freely flows. Open divine doors. Send kingdom connections. Awaken dreams that have gone dormant. Break every chain that tries to keep her from soaring.

Seal Your Word deep within her. Let it bear fruit in due season. May she rise as Your Royal Diadem—glorious, unshakable, and anchored in You.

In the mighty name of Jesus,

Amen.

ABOUT THE AUTHOR

Apostle Chiquista Dornell, aka Queen Chi, is a Prophetic Voice, EmpowHerment Coach, and Spiritual Midwife to women rising in faith and purpose. Join her *Queen Mogul Empire*—a sacred community of prayer, business, and sisterhood—at www.iamqueenme.com, and awaken the royal within.

CONNECTING IN SPIRIT

Connecting with the Eagles International Training Institute (EITI) was a blessing unknown to man but known to our creator. While visiting my family and friends one Christmas holiday, I spoke with my childhood friend Alicia Burnette about the dance ministry in Atlanta, and she connected me with her dance instructor, the late Myrah McKenni, from her church. She discovered that her contact was Eagle Dr. Kina Nichols (Arnold). Eagle Kina came to my grandparents' home, and I purchased her book, *The Priesthood of Dance*, and she told me about the EITI. Upon returning home to Georgia, I contacted the state representative at the time, Eagle Tatanya Aker (Mason), and the connection to The Eagle Network (TEN) and the EITI began.

During year two of TEN, there was a shift. An unfortunate car accident tried to stop me from completing my last module for graduation. *"I can do all things through Christ who strengthens me"* (Philippians 4:13 NKJV). Standing on the Word of God, Apostle Scott permitted me to continue with the module one-on-

one and to omit the dance because of my injuries. It was nothing but the grace of God. I completed and graduated from Georgia.

After graduation, a lot of things occurred in my life. I was able to go through dance year one to finally become an Eagle. Later, I taught TEN and assisted with the Lions International Training Institute (LITI) Culinary—a fantastic journey teaching the foundation of dance and other areas. The EITI changed my life and allowed me to delve deeper into studying the Word of God and teaching other individuals. I introduced ten other young ladies into the dance ministry. Some dance at their churches, but none have accepted the calling of an Eagle. I am grateful to have changed lives and provided a foundation. In addition to Dance Year One, I have completed the Eagles International Authors Institute (EIAI) Year One. In 2017, I wrote two books: *Who Are You Listening To? Developing the Leader in You* and *Write the Vision: A 50-Day Journey Journal*. In 2019, I wrote *Nation2Nation Entrepreneurs Making Bold Moves*; in 2020, I wrote *Expats: What They Don't Tell You*; and in 2025, *Caring for the Queen: A Daughter's Love*. Grateful to the EIAI!

To SOAR, one must understand the various accounts; you must search within your soul and seek God for guidance and direction before you can excel when you SOAR. After accepting my call in the liturgical dance ministry as an Eagle, I understood what soaring meant. It involves laying down my tendency to thrive. Learning to use less energy to get people to love me, I started pouring that energy into myself. According to Isaiah 40:31 (NLT), *"But those who trust in the LORD will find new strength. They will soar high on wings like eagles. They will run and not grow weary. They will walk and not faint."*

I am humble to receive and grateful to all the teachers in my life for lessons soaring in ministry and life.

LESSONS FROM SOARING

In 2017, while writing as the Holy Spirit instructed me, I experienced a spiritual and mental transformation. *Who Are You Listening To? Developing the Leader in You* spoke volumes to my life process and throughout the EITI. As a single parent, I had to learn not to listen to so much parental advice from others. I learned not to listen to the crowds and stand out in the crowd of murmurs. It is not about my past but how God moves me closer to my destiny. The book discusses how God changed Moses, Paul, Deborah, Lydia, and others while they were on the path to becoming leaders to be impactful to many. While writing my summary, Holy Spirit told me about my second book, *Write the Vision: A 50-Day Journey Journal*. This journal is about scriptures filled with blank pages for readers to take a spiritual journey as they draw closer to God. In 2018, my new chapter in life began. I turned 50 and left the known to travel to the unknown in China. A twelve-year vision.

Living in China was more than just a vision and a dream; it allowed me to let go and listen closely to God. I learned more about myself and realized that I was ENOUGH.

> "... and then he told me, My grace is enough; it's all you need. My strength comes into its own in your weakness. Once I heard that, I was glad to let it happen. I quit focusing on the handicap and began appreciating the gift. It was a case of Christ's strength moving in on my weakness." (2 Corinthians 12:9 MSG).

God allowed me to SOAR in another country, and as I soared, I found my voice again. God allowed me to start an international devotional ministry on WeChat, Hope, Heal, and Agape.

Healing and Agape. So many individuals are in the group who are broken on the inside. Some are striving to thrive and become closer to God; others are learning to heal through scripture and let go of their anger. China has allowed me to SOAR in my writing as well. The Holy Spirit allowed me to connect to a broken system through Expats. The book is called *Expats: What They Don't Tell You*. When accepting the contract to teach at an international school, they did not inform me of any financial matters or about the school itself. Of course, there are not a lot of resources or other individuals to contact for verification, like in the United States. Although all went well initially, I did not know the school was a training school. It was an after-school program for Chinese students to learn English and enhance other academic subjects they needed to excel in.

In addition, there was a hidden racial aspect in their marketing, amongst other things. Not all bad, but there are some very good things to know, such as social security that is paid to you after you leave from some schools; thus, some international schools are set up like the states with paid time off. In addition, there are rules about being able to have an overseas business. Another opportunity came about while living in Qingdao, China. After meeting several expat business owners, another book arose from that experience, *Nation2Nation Entrepreneurs Making Bold Moves*. I contacted my Eagle sisters and other friends in the United States to participate in this book. I did my first International Book tour with various entrepreneurs globally telling their stories of how they all got started in business. These are all part of Soaring's application. The EIAI taught me to expand beyond my circle. Are you willing to grow beyond your circle, step out, and trust God to move to another country or state? What is holding you back from soaring?

We all have distractions in our lives and people who are in our circle that we need to let go of; and we need to start listening to God. Surround yourself with like-minded people, or join groups that have the same interests. You must allow yourself to be teachable, reflect upon what you have been taught, and apply it in your life journey. It is not too late. Imagine a life filled with joy, peace, and financial security today. Then, imagine *you* in that place.

Now, after 20 years, I have returned to my birth home to care for my mother and brother. In 2023, I earned my doctorate while serving as a full-time caregiver. In January 2025, I received the Lifetime Presidential Award under the former President Joseph Biden. I completed a Certified Public Speaking course and am now doing an international virtual book tour from May to August 2025. I am connecting to the Spirit and Soaring as a single mother, liturgical dancer, author, ordained minister, worshipper, caregiver, and entrepreneur. When connected to God through the Holy Spirit, you can soar beyond anything you could imagine.

ABOUT THE AUTHOR

Rev. Dr. Charisse R. Drakeford, a native of Chicago, Illinois, is a devoted mother to Mya and a caregiver to her mother. She is an entrepreneur, author, certified public speaker, Notary Near Me Illinois.COM, LLC owner, and recipient of a 2025 Presidential Lifetime Achievement Award (BWWWM).

No Limits ~ No Boundaries ~ No Fear

THE ALTAR WHERE MY DANCE BEGAN – THE ALTAR WHERE MY DANCE BELONGS

Introduction

I have been called to help and assist dancers/dance ministers by teaching dance techniques to help enhance the gift God has already given them. If I can assist with providing more structure to their bodies, which can produce more confidence, it will help the dance minister to focus less on the technique and more on the worship.

> *"There I will go to the altar of God, to God—the source of all my joy. I will praise you with my harp, O God, my God!"* (Psalm 43:4 NLT).

The First Dance
(Childhood & Catholic School)

As a child, I went to a Catholic school in Philadelphia, Pennsylvania. When I was in approximately the fourth grade, one of the nuns (Sister Mark) asked me if I wanted to participate in the Easter play. After I agreed, she told me to ask my parents to buy ballet slippers because she was going to teach me "a dance." Sister Mark, who was not yet a confirmed nun but a sister-in-training at the time, was the first African American "sister" I had ever met. It was great to have a young Christian woman, who looked somewhat like me, spending time mentoring me and training me to do my first dance.

I met with Sister Mark after school, and she taught me a dance to the song, "I Don't Know How to Love Him," from the Broadway play Jesus Christ Superstar. This was a song about Mary Magdalene, where Jesus changed her life, and how she finally knew what true love was. She turned out to be one of Jesus' greatest disciples! The dance involved me washing Jesus' feet, and after the play was over, I fell in love with dance immediately. I then asked my mother if I could go to dance school. I would like to mention this was the 1970s, and dancing on the altar was not something that was done, especially in a Catholic church. I was the first student at the school and member of the church to ever do so in the church's history! It was after this event I felt such a closeness to God and could sense His presence, especially at night when I lay in bed. To this day I do not know what made her choose me out of all the students, but all I can say is it was all God!

My love for dance exploded! If anyone was looking for me, they could always find me in a dance class—in grade school, junior high school, and high school. I danced with the Modern Dance Club at my local community center, and at a local dance studio. When I enrolled in high school, I auditioned at, was accepted by, and attended the Philadelphia High School for Creative and Performing Arts. I was trained in ballet, jazz, and Horton modern dance, and I also had classes in drama, voice, dance improvisation, and more. It was such an exciting time in my life! I also danced and was a cheerleader in college; however, I stopped dancing for many years, devoting my time to being a wife and mother.

The Return to the Altar (Reconnection in CT/MA)

My family and I moved to Connecticut, where I dedicated my life to the Lord around 1987, and we later moved to Springfield, MA, in 1997. I joined a church there, where the pastor's wife found out I was a dancer and dance teacher, and she asked if I would participate in the Resurrection Day service by ministering in dance. I agreed, and she told me she wanted me to be Mary Magdalene and wash Jesus' feet! The look that I gave her ... All I knew was I'd had the same experience as a child. After I ministered in dance for Resurrection Day, I never stopped dancing.

I don't think it was a coincidence that I was asked to do the same dance, portraying the same biblical character, for the same purpose. God reminded me that my first dance was not done in a dance studio or on a stage—the art of dance was introduced to me in a church, and my first dance was on the ALTAR. On the altar is where dance began for me, and the altar is where my dance belongs!

After moving to Connecticut in 1987 and re-pursuing dance in the mid-90s, I knew it had to be the Lord when I was given the opportunity to minister in dance at my former church. I realized how much I had missed my passion but lacked the knowledge and foundation of dance ministry. I did not know anyone in my area who had knowledge of or taught dancing as worship. So, I spent a great deal of time on the internet and discovered "Christian dance" was alive and well, especially on the West Coast. I researched what dance in worship was, about garments and where to find them, what the colors meant, what the instruments symbolized, and more.

The Journey of the Eagle (Searching, Training, TEN/EITI)

One day while on the internet, I ran across a woman by the name of Pamela Rutherford, who had a dance ministry and travel itinerary and who was coming to Cambridge, Massachusetts, to teach. I drove 1.5 hours to the church where she was, and I watched this beautiful woman give her testimony and talk about what dancing for the Lord meant. She then demonstrated movement to us, and I could not believe I'd finally found someone who could talk to me about this joy and love that I felt when I danced in the Lord's presence! When it was time for everyone to dance, I was in such awe that I was glued to my seat and just sat and watched. I did, however, purchase her manual, and I've had it ever since.

> *"For every one that asketh receiveth; and he that seeketh findeth; and to him that knocketh it shall be opened"* (Matthew 7:8 KJV).

I was hungry for the Word and the role dance played. I took time to attend conferences over the years, traveling alone to places like New York, the Bahamas, and Texas. I was determined to learn more, and it was exciting to meet other hungry dance ministers who wanted to learn and have fellowship as well. Unfortunately, every time I came back to New England, there was no one I could talk to about my experiences or who could truly understand what I had learned or seen. My previous church did not allow dancers to worship freely in the sanctuary, only special presentations, so my gift/calling just lay dormant until I went to another workshop or conference. I felt like this Eagle was flying around for wisdom and knowledge, trying to eat up all that I could, but I had no like-minded people in my life to talk to or have fellowship with.

As the early 2000s approached, I was still dancing and searching, and still there was nothing offered in my area, until one day I heard about TEN Worldwide. This time, I drove two hours to Boston, Massachusetts, to learn more. It was about 2011 when I experienced the first module, and I met people who shared the same love and passion for Dance in the Lord. They were there to gain the same knowledge and understanding I was seeking. It was so refreshing!

> *"Then make my joy complete by being like-minded, having the same love, being one in spirit and of one mind"* (Philippians 2:2 NIV).

When the Eagles/teachers started talking to us about the Eagles International Training Institute (EITI) and the founder, Apostle Dr. Pamela Scott, it dawned on me that it was the same Pamela Rutherford that I had seen long ago in Cambridge, Massachusetts! Everything had come full circle, and only God knew our paths would cross again! I believe it was a divine connection.

I continued attending the modules through TEN Worldwide and graduated from TEN Dance Year 1 in 2012 and Dance Year 2 in 2013. I served as a TEN assistant in 2014, always driving two hours from my home to be around the TEN students and my Eagle family that was teaching us. I was not alone anymore. I was surrounded by Eagles who flocked together and were soaring! I was then prompted to become a teacher/Eagle, and I enrolled in EITI and graduated from Dance Year 1, becoming a licensed dance minister. Would you believe the same manual I purchased so many years ago was the same manual for the Dance Year 1 course? What Apostle Pamela teaches and ministers is consistent and has never changed.

I educated myself more at EITI by graduating from Choregeo, a dance leadership course, in 2022, and the authors' school in 2023, where I wrote my first book. Because of EITI and the leadership of Apostle Dr. Pamela Scott, I continue to meet more Eagles, and I can go just about anywhere in the world and look for an Eagle and be able to meet them wherever they are: the Caribbean islands, Korea, Cuba, Suriname, Puerto Rico, and more! We were all trained the same, and we are connected as a family. A world full of Eagles that soar!

> *"They that wait upon the Lord shall renew their strength; they shall mount up with wings as eagles; they shall run, and not be weary; and they shall walk, and not faint"* (Isaiah 40:31 KJV).

The Birth of Smooth Stone Dance (Ministry Formation)

In 2009, I saw a dance ministry minister on a local public TV station in Springfield, and I was elated! I met the dance arts pastor and was hired to teach dance (ballet and modern dance) to their dance ministry teams: dancers, mime, and flaggers—from small children to adults. I looked forward to teaching them because they were hungry to learn. I would periodically attend their church to check on their progress, and boy, did their dance change! They looked more confident, graceful—freer! God then let me know that I was called to help the dance minister perfect the gift of dance they had already been given so that they could minister in a more excellent way. The joy I felt being around the dancers, the congregation, and the Word brought forth by the ministry led me to become a member of Crossover Church (formerly Apostolic Renewal Church), of which I am still a member. There is so much freedom in worship and dance there! Hallelujah!

> *"Now the Lord is that Spirit: and where the Spirit of the Lord is, there is liberty"* (2 Corinthians 3:17 KJV).

Smooth Stone Dance Consortium/Ministry came to be when I went back to college to complete my bachelor's degree in 2009; I graduated in 2011. I have a degree in social science with a concentration in sociology and psychology. As part of my college internship, I taught modern dance at a local community center. During this time, I was also teaching at a well-known local dance studio and at another dance studio that served low-income families.

Throughout the years, I had been giving personal lessons at my home studio as well as traveling to students' locations. When I saw people were requesting the lessons, and most either could not get to a dance studio or could not afford it, I purchased a 13-foot portable ballet barre, and I would bring the dance studio to the people at their locations. I created a mobile dance studio! My business turned into a consortium, where I was teaching private lessons and group lessons at my home, someone else's home, and online via Zoom teleconferencing.

The Call to Excellence (Theological Framework & Book)

My business transformed and coincided with dance ministry in that not only was I sharing it with my church at one point, but I was also being asked to teach at other churches with dance teams or individuals and at workshops and conferences. I found that I have been used greatly with beginners' ballet and beginners' Horton modern dance, which gives me the chance to take untrained dancers especially and help mold and transform their bodies to help with their grace, balance, poise, and body alignment. I also teach dancers who are already trained and take classes as a refresher. In both scenarios, I find it totally rewarding that I can be of benefit, helping others in their quest to dance for the Lord in excellence.

> "Show yourself in all respects to be a model of good works, and in your teaching show integrity, dignity…" (Titus 2:7 ESV).

Over the years, I unfortunately ran into people who had reasons or excuses as to why dance technique classes were not important to the dancer, specifically the dance minister. I was prompted by the Lord to write a book on a subject that I knew was not always talked about, nor had I seen a book written about it. In 2023, I wrote the book *The Dance Minister and Dance Technique: What God Says About Skill*. I wanted to share that God could of course use anyone trained and untrained to do what He wanted, but why not be greatly skilled at something where He could use you specifically for an even greater work or assignment? Noah is a great example of a skilled carpenter who God used to build the ark in preparation for the great flood.

Why would the dance minister not want to perfect their gift so that they can minister more in excellence? I could not get past the thought that if musicians individually and corporately would practice their craft, and singers would individually and corporately practice as well, then why not the dance minister? I would often share this example with people: If you were to gain a promotion at your job with a better title and salary, and you had to take courses to prepare for that, most would jump at the chance, so why not for the Lord?

"Study to shew thyself approved unto God, a workman that needeth not to be ashamed, rightly dividing the word of truth" (2 Timothy 2:15 KJV).

Final Admonition
(Encouragement for Dance Ministers)

As we continue to strive to be our very best for God and others, we must remember the qualities of an eagle. They adapt to flight; they spread their wings to lift and fly, and eagles are hunters that dive toward the things they desire. They are also survivors.[1] Where we start is not always where things will end. Despite the circumstances, people, and things that may come, we must keep pressing through to accomplish all God has for us. Have faith, learn all you can, and listen to His instructions. Soar above it all and win!

References:

[1] How Do Eagles Fly? Revealing the Secrets of Their Soaring

ABOUT THE AUTHOR

Gina M. Emanuel-Satchell—dancer, teacher, choreographer, licensed dance minister, and author of *The Dance Minister and Dance Technique: What God Says About Skill*. She is the founder of Smooth Stone Dance Consortium/Ministry, an on-site/online dance class. Gina teaches dancers, dance ministers, dance ministry teams, and dance workshops and conferences.

SERVING TO SOAR

Out of the Comfort Zone, Into the Yes

1 Samuel 3:10 KJV

"And the LORD came, and stood, and called as at other times, Samuel, Samuel. Then Samuel answered, Speak; for thy servant heareth."

Isaiah 6:8 KJV

"Also I heard the voice of the Lord, saying, Whom shall I send, and who will go for us? Then said I, Here am I; send me."

In the Beginning

Since the early days of my faith walk, I purposed in my heart to yield to God in every way possible. While I have grown in this area of yielding, after almost four decades of growing in and walking by faith, I still have not arrived; nor do I get it right all of the time (Philippians 3:13). As those of us who may be more mature in the faith may realize, and those of us who are not as mature will soon find out, when you tell God, "Yes," when you yield to Him, He takes you on some journeys that will cause you to soar and will result in you assisting others in soaring. This is usually filled with discomfort, yet it is fully worth it.

One such season in my life is connected to my call to intercession. I come from a heritage of intercessors: My maternal grandmother and my mother are great prayer warriors, women of fervent prayer. Upon initiating my faith walk and accepting salvation, I did not fathom that I would be in line for such a heritage. In fact, that was furthest from my mind. While I was more than grateful for the great exchange of my unrighteousness to become the righteousness of God (2 Corinthians 5:21), I was also more than content playing background. Because of my heritage, prayer was a significant part of my life growing up and even more so once I accepted Jesus as my Savior. Early in my faith walk, I would spend long stints in intercession privately. That habit would later sometimes spill over publicly. However, in the early years of my faith walk, this was not a comfortable place for me publicly.

As a young Christian fresh out of college and entering into the workforce with little more than five years of salvation under my girding belt (Ephesians 6:14), I obediently went where God told me to go in secular ministry. Faithful Father God provided sound people of faith around me. I had the pleasure and blessing of having people of faith, brothers and sisters in Christ, in my workplace.

Opportunities to grow my faith and to impact the world around me, to be the light and the salt that He has called for us to be (Matthew 5:13-16), soon arose. This was not at all comfortable for me. I tend to be more of an introvert, so I am usually reserved. I did spend a lot of time in prayer, in fellowship with Holy Spirit, and receiving instruction from the Word of God. Little did I realize that these were times of receiving strategy and discipline, of being called out and chosen (Matthew 22:14; Ephesians 1) and of having it be made blatantly apparent that I was a peculiar people and a royal priesthood (1 Peter 2:9).

Uncomfortable Stretching: The Assignment

It was initially here that God began to use me in both unusual and uncomfortable ways. During my quiet times of prayer, Holy Spirit would give me the faces or names of coworkers, and I would pray for them. Later, He began to give me specific instructions and prayers to pray for some of my coworkers and some of those that I served in my workplace. I would be amazed and pleasantly surprised when I would hear praise reports of the very thing God had given me for someone in prayer. Initially, I rarely shared these amazing occurrences with others, wondering if anyone would believe me or if others had similar experiences.

Gradually, much to my surprise at that time, Holy Spirit added more and began to sometimes give me instructions that required me to take action: to call one of my coworkers, to speak a word of encouragement, to speak a word of knowledge to a family, or to speak a word of wisdom to someone (though I did not know the proper terms for these back then). He would occasionally give me warnings for some as well.

Sad to say, my initial response was great hesitation, and I found excuses as to why I should not approach others or why the timing was poor. As Holy Spirit began to reveal that those inclinations did indeed come from Him and that I had missed opportunities when I neglected to obey, I began to resolve to allow Him to help me overcome fear.

Expansion

A short time later, when I began to be more comfortable with the intercession and tasks that Holy Spirit led me in concerning my workplace, He decided to take me through another level of intercession, submission, and obedience. One of my coworkers was an older woman who worked as a security guard. She was a woman of God who I often saw reading the Bible at work. I later learned that she was titled a missionary in her local church. She came to me one day and asked me to pray with her. She also asked me to touch the part of her body that was in pain at the time. I was quite shocked and a little taken aback. I could not, at the time, fathom why she would ask me to pray. She had many more years of salvation than I. I had not yet learned about prayers of agreement or laying hands on the sick. I had only seen licensed ministers do so. I could not find it in my heart or spirit to say no to her plea, though inside fear attempted to rise up. I complied and prayed the only way I knew how, as if I were in my intimate quiet time with God.

Much to my shock and surprise, as we closed in prayer, she began to state how much better she felt. She began rejoicing and praising right there at work. I was further floored, but out of respect, I quietly rejoiced with her and thanked God for using me.

I had a very candid conversation with Father God as I went back to my area. I could not understand why He needed me to be the one selected to carry out the assignment. I felt blindsided. When I later got to spend quiet time with the Lord, He simply responded, why not me? I had an extensive list of reasons why not. However, at the end of my list, God asked me if I loved Him. I answered in the affirmative. He then asked me if I loved His people. I answered that I had to because He commanded that we do. His response indicated that I would then carry out whatever He asked me to do on the behalf of others. I could not argue, of course, and it negated every excuse I wanted to give.

Serving Into Soaring

I should not have been surprised that this was only the first of many similar occurrences. But I was. Other coworkers would ask me to pray with them on occasion. A number of our faith brothers and sisters would come and ask me to pray for them for varying reasons. After the candid conversation with God and Him negating my list of excuses, I could never say no. I would be quite surprised that they would call on me for prayer. I wondered why they were asking me to pray for them. Why were they seeking me out? Why did they want my help? I struggled to understand why people of God, who had many years more than me in faith or who had ministry titles, would ask me to pray for them or with them. I knew no better than to say yes to whatever God instructed and allowed. I had no confidence in my ability to make any impact. However, I learned that I did not need confidence in myself, only in God, in His omniscience, in His omnipotence, and in His love for us. These experiences launched me into a new level of intercession, into a new level of dependence on and confidence in God, that caused my faith to grow by leaps and bounds.

The Word of God tells us in Isaiah 40:31 (KJV), *"But they that wait upon the Lord shall renew their strength."*

In the original Hebrew text, the phrase *"they that wait upon"* is the word *qavah*. In *Strong's Exhaustive Concordance and Bible Dictionary*, the word *qavah* is referenced as Hebrew reference number 6960 with the following definition:

"To wait, to look for, to hope, to expect; meaning to bind together, collect."

Biblehub.com expounds on the use of the verb *qavah*:

"... primarily conveys the idea of waiting with anticipation or hope. It is often used in the context of looking forward to something with eager expectation. This waiting is not passive but involves confident expectation of God's intervention or fulfillment of His promises. The term can also imply a sense of gathering or binding together, as in the intertwining of strands to form a cord, symbolizing strength and unity."

The site goes on to describe the cultural and historical background of the use of this verb *qavah*.

"In ancient Hebrew culture, waiting was often associated with faith and trust in God's timing and provision. The agrarian society of ancient Israel required patience and reliance on God for the growth of crops and the provision of rain. This cultural context underscores the spiritual discipline of waiting on the Lord, which is a recurring theme throughout the Hebrew Scriptures. The concept of "*qavah*" reflects a deep-seated belief in God's faithfulness and sovereignty."

The definition of the word "wait" in my language (American English) resonates within the context of this Scripture as well. The *Merriam-Webster Dictionary* yields three definitions of the transitive verb "wait":

1. to stay in place in expectation of: await
2. to delay serving (a meal)
3. to act as a server for

For me, that *"wait upon the Lord"* in that season of growth was all of the above.

- The "wait" was a "look for" Faithful Abba Father God to help me overcome fear and doubt (Romans 8:14-15; 2 Timothy 1:7).

- The "wait" was "hope" in God's Word and His precious promises (Numbers 23:19; Psalm 119:89; Isaiah 40:8; 55:11).

- The "wait" was an "expectation" that His grace was sufficient, that His strength would be made perfect in my weakness

(2 Corinthians 12:9) and that His promises were sure (2 Corinthians 1:20).

- The "wait" was a "binding together" of my faith with that of my fellow believers, allowing Holy Spirit to add His super to our natural, producing manifestation (Ecclesiastes 4:12; Matthew 18:18-20).
- The "wait" was "collecting" the praise reports proving God's faithfulness and love (Psalm 34:8; 27:13-14).
- The "wait" was a "stay in the place" of submission and obedience to God "in expectation of" His will being done and His plan being executed (Psalm 42:11; 62:5).
- The "wait" was a "delay" in "serving" my own selfish desires and comfort (starving doubt and unbelief while feeding my faith, better known as fasting or abstention) (Matthew 17:21; Mark 9:29; Galatians 5:16, 25).
- The "wait" was "acting as a server" for God, attending to His desires and the desires of others, at the Master's beck and call (Matthew 20:26-28; 25:23; Mark 10:43-45; Colossians 3:23-24).

Worth It All

This was one of many of the seasons along the journey to renewed strength and to mounting and soaring. There is discomfort, adjustment, sacrifice, and reward to the shifts we are brought to and brought through along the journey to soaring. As in the natural changing altitudes of ascension and rising to the heights Faithful Abba Father calls us to in the spirit, soaring requires another level of grace: new lung capacity (*ruach*, breath,

Isaiah 25:4; Ezekiel 37:9-10), stretching and expansion (wings spread wide, out of comfort zones, enlarging territory / building capacity, Isaiah 54:2-3), expanded eyesight and perspective (seeing from above, God-focals on, Isaiah 55:8-9; Mark 8:25). Every shift is worth the discomfort and the necessary learning curves. It teaches us the immediate and courageous obedience and yieldedness to our Faithful Father launching us into the destiny of our Kingdom citizenship and bringing others along with us.

Will you allow Faithful Father God to take you out of your current place of comfort into your next level of immediate and courageous obedience (Joshua 1:9)? Will you give Him another "yes" (Isaiah 6:8)? Waiting on Him in service to others will take you to soaring heights beyond what you can ask or imagine (Ephesians 3:20), launching you into the destination (destiny) He has planned for you all along (Romans 8:29-30; Ephesians 2:10). Give God your "yes," no matter how uncomfortable the next level may be.

Find more anointed encouragement to soaring with affirming scripture messages in the three-volume Affirm Series by Consuelo Gaines:

Affirm Greatness Realize Destiny, Affirm Greatness Realize Success, and *Affirm Kids.*

ABOUT THE AUTHOR

Consuelo Gaines is a licensed educator, administrator, speaker, author, entrepreneur, and servant-leader with over four decades of service to families in the private and public education sectors across nations. Since receiving salvation, she has flourished in biblical study and ministry and shares this with others around the globe.

CROSSING OVER

"*The one who had escaped came and told Abram the Hebrew ...*" (Genesis 14:13 NKJV). The root letters of the word "Hebrew" mean "from the other side, the other side, or beyond." When we say we are going to the other side, there has to be a crossing-over. If I use the words "crossed over," it means that we have arrived, but when we use the words "crossing over," it means we have not come to the end of the journey; we are still on it.

In studying his life, it becomes clear that Abram was always on a journey, whether physically or in experience. As Abram, we are on a constant journey in our walk and experience with God. I want to share my experience with the Eagles International Training Institute as part of my journey. It will be a challenge and a blessing and will change your life.

The Invitation I Didn't Want

I came to know about the EITI in 2016; Apostle Pamela and a team were invited to the Island of Aruba by a member of another congregation for a conference. Somehow, the plans did not turn out as planned, and we were asked if we could open our church doors to host the conference. Hesitant, I opened the doors but decided not to attend. They would have the conference and be charged for using the facility when it was finished. But as they started, I was uncomfortable not attending and hearing what was happening, so I decided to participate. I sat and observed, and at the end of the first meeting, I observed when Apostle Pamela, whom I had not met personally, was asking in a low voice: "Who is that individual? Is that the pastor or the one who organized the conference?" With that, I decided to walk up to the team and introduce myself as the pastor of this local assembly. I said to them, "Please make yourselves at home," and with that, I left. The conference was a success.

The Worship That Undid Me

I was asked if Apostle Janine Dailey could minister on Sunday morning at our church and Apostle Pamela at the church that organized the conference. The crossing-over began during worship. Apostle Janine Dailey made everyone push back the chairs, called everyone forward, and demonstrated what every individual had to do to dance, something we were not accustomed to doing. It came together, and we had good worship and preaching, but now then we had to dismantle the seating accommodation, dancing, and push back the enemy. What I experienced left something with me that made me want more, and it moved us away from the norm of what we were accustomed to doing.

In 2017, we held a conference here on the Island with Apostle Pamela, which, as a church, we hosted. It was later in the same year that we traveled to the EITI Summit for the first time. That was a blast for my wife and me; we had never seen anything like it. The worship was not what we were accustomed to; dancers were out with flags and banners, and the joy and oneness displayed was an experience we had never seen before. There was such anointing in that room; we were just looking at each other because we had never experienced this before. Seeing the intercessors on the floor interceding before the meeting started was lovely and impactful. Returning to our hotel room, our topic was worship, and we loved it.

This was where our journey in crossing over continued because we felt like we could stay in that experience. God allowed us to be there in that conference to take us on a journey that we did not fully understand, but if we were willing to follow Him in it, we would experience what we had never experienced before in crossing over. This experience has brought a change even in our time of worship, prayer, and intercession within our congregation; we trusted the Lord to implement some things we had experienced. All that I have shared has been part of our crossing-over, our "Abram the Hebrew" experience. You might be in a similar place and not recognize yourself on a constant journey in the Lord and with Him; I do trust, as we continue, you will be able to cross over into your place with God.

From Refusal to Revelation

A couple of years after that time, someone challenged me to take a course with the EITI. I was also asked, "Are you afraid?" I said no, I was not scared, but I felt in my heart and asked, "Why should I take a course when I have already been through three years of hard training in Guyana?" My attitude was that I had what

I needed to know, and I was okay with that. I could not get away from what was suggested, so I began to pray and ask the Lord what I should do. Immediately, the word that came to me was to take up the study of Kingdom Spheres, and you can guess who the teacher of that class was: Apostle Pamela. This was another phase of my crossing-over; my studies in Guyana differed from the setting I was going through, so I had to make a significant adjustment in my mindset. One of my first experiences was having to do lots of reading, and one of the first books was *A Shift in Leadership* by Apostle John Eckhart. As I read, I began to feel that this was not what I knew, and I came to the place of wanting to push away the material dealing with my position as the church pastor. In pushing away the material, I told the Lord, "Lord, if you don't deal with my mind, I will quit this study right now."

The Shift in My Thinking

Did He answer me? Oh yes, He did. He said to take the material, continue through it, and go through all of it because my change was about to take place. I was on the verge of crossing over from my stand on how the church should be to what the Lord was to reveal to me. As senior pastor, I thought that I was the one who had the ultimate plan and that my position was that of the leading man, only to learn how the Lord's setting was established in the church. Then, the other lesson I had to know was that of the Kingdom; we have learned so much about the church and how we believe the church should be, and we have learned nothing or very little about the Kingdom. So, when I speak about crossing over, these were some of the experiences I have had in crossing over from one mindset to another; it was not easy to get to the other side. I went through the entire course, and I thank the Lord for having changed my mindset from being pastoral to the mentality of being apostolic. If you are reading this testimony and are in the pastoral leadership mindset, I encourage you to be open to the Lord for what He wants to reveal regarding the next phase of your ministry and your walk with Him. I have seen individuals who have rejected change and are satisfied to stay in what they are accustomed to. I have been there, but as I learned and saw through being involved in studying Kingdom Spheres, I realized that God was doing much more than we think and believe. He is bringing His leaders into a new dimension of operating within their ministry by bringing expansion to His Kingdom.

From 1986, the year my wife and I were ordained as pastors, to 2018, I operated in one way, in what I believed and how many others think it should be done. Still, as I took up the challenge to learn, I began to learn what the Lord was doing, which was nothing new because this is how the Lord Jesus moved with His disciples in equipping them to expand His Kingdom here on Earth. For me, it was new because I did not know what the Lord was doing through men and women who had the revelation and the understanding and were willing to take steps of faith in moving into that revelation of crossing over.

I do not pull down where I was and the mentality I walked in because that was all I knew, but I was willing to take the risk to cross over and open myself to learn what the Lord was doing in His Kingdom. Now I have come into a Kingdom mindset, in which I am still growing and want to continue to grow; we call that "Soaring." Did I finish my course in Kingdom Spheres? Oh yes, I did, and I learned a lot, for which I am grateful.

Called to Teach

When I thought it was over, and now I could settle in, my experience of crossing being over, the Lord was saying He had another shocker for me. One day, I was sitting in my office awaiting an apostle working in Australia. When WhatsApp buzzed on my phone, I looked at it, and there was a message from Apostle Pamela. When I opened the message, Apostle Pamela asked me to become an instructor at the school of ministry within the EITI. I was so shocked that I began to speak to myself and say that I knew nothing about teaching in an institute. I wanted to be refreshed by attending the EITI Summit, and now it had become more than that. Now, it had become crossing over to teach in something larger than standing in a church building and teaching the people I knew, which was my comfort zone.

I came home before giving Apostle Pamela the answer and spoke to my wife, who asked if I would accept the challenge. You never know what the Lord will do when you begin to open yourself to get ready to cross over. He often takes you into the unknown. I told my wife hesitantly, "Yes, I will do it." Then, she told me to accept the challenge. So, I said yes to Apostle Pamela, that it would be a pleasure to do it, and I asked if she could send me the material. The answer I received was, "You have to develop your material."

You who are reading this can imagine how I felt: She had asked me to teach, and now I had to come up with my material. I was ready to throw in the towel even before I started, but there is something that I saw in the apostle, and that was that God had given her the ability to pull out of you that which is hidden and dormant within. When I told my wife what was said to me, she turned to me and said, "Well, I want to challenge you to sit, take your Bible, and come up with that which the Lord will give you to teach."

Again, you see a crossing over to the other side from where you are accustomed to being (Soaring). I accepted the challenge. That night, I went to sleep with a pad and a pen at my bedside, and I told the Lord I had never done this, but if this is where He was leading me, then I was ready to receive what He would give me to put together. The Lord came through that night by downloading the characters' names in scripture and told me, "You are going to teach on the character of these individuals, who the Lord called to fulfill a purpose." So I had to jump out of my sleep and put the characters' names on paper and study them to pass on to the students who would attend classes. I consider this crossing over and soaring into another dimension because I had never been there before. For me, this was the beginning of some new things that were taking place in my life. Just when you think you are coming to settle down in your ministry, the Lord comes and stirs your nest because He wants you to cross over and soar.

Crossing Into the Unknown

Was this the end of my crossing over? The answer is no. As I said before, the apostle has a way of pulling out of you or awakening that which is dormant within you. About one year ago, the Doctor of Ministry (DMin) was to begin. This was at the heart of the apostle for a long time, and it finally started. Someone asked me if I would join the classes, and my answer was no. Soon after, I was invited to a Zoom meeting, not knowing what it was all about. When I attended the meeting, the discussion started on the DMin classes, that I was to be one of the teachers who would be teaching, and what I would be teaching.

I sat there, quietly listening to all that was being said, being open to the Lord about what He wanted to do in and through me. In this journey of crossing over, I have learned that you do not ask the Lord where we are going, but you trust Him. As before, I asked the apostle what I should teach, and the apostle shared an idea with me. I had but a short time to make preparations, but as I gave myself, the Lord helped me and gave me a download and helped in my research to develop the material. This was another crossing-over moment for me, journeying from one place to another. And the journey is not what you are accustomed to taking; it is one where you have to trust the Lord and be open. I have never been on a crossing-over journey like this. The Lord has always taught me never to stop trusting Him. I want to challenge you, who are reading this chapter, and ask you a question. What is it that the Lord is speaking to you that you are afraid to obey? Just look back at Abram when he was called in Genesis 12; he was already on a journey in chapter 11 when his father died and left them. This was God's opportunity for the Lord who had His eyes on Abram to make the call to begin the crossing-over process so that it would come to its fullness.

What Has to Die for You to Cross Over?

What has to die in you so that you will hear the Divine voice of God calling you to take this crossing-over journey?"

ABOUT THE AUTHOR

 I am Tomasito Gibbs. I am from the Island of Aruba. I attended Bible School in Guyana for three years. Before returning home, I married my wife, Victoria, who is also from the Island of Aruba. We labored together in our home church and were ordained as senior pastors on August 10th, 1986.

TRIALS TO TRIUMPHS: THE UNTOLD LESSONS

My experience at the Eagles International Training Institute has been truly remarkable. I am of the firm conviction that I was directed to this path by a higher power, which has transformed my perception from that of a mere dancer to that of a woman who has been selected to assist others in breaking free from cycles of perplexity and discovering their authentic selves. I am genuinely appreciative of God for facilitating that. On this day, I would like to extend an invitation to you to accompany me as I contemplate my personal transformation and the way I am embracing my authentic purpose. I am experiencing a sensation akin to that of a soaring eagle, and this time, I am confident that it is all part of a divine plan. This experience has had a profound impact on my life, and I am confident that by sharing it with you, you will also experience a positive transformation.

The Call

In 2015, I was extended a wonderful invitation to become a member of the Ten Worldwide network, a community that is committed to imparting dance principles in person. I now understand that the invitation was merely the commencement of my new journey. I was already deeply involved in dancing at that juncture in my life; however, becoming a dance teacher was a concept that I had never encountered.

Truthfully, I failed to recognize that this experience was merely the beginning of a much more significant endeavor. I must confess that I was largely unaware of the true meaning of kingdom ministry during my childhood, as I was raised in a traditional church environment. I commenced my voyage with the conviction that I was merely a dancer, as I believed that was the only way I was destined to express myself. In year one, I embarked on my voyage with EITI dance with the primary objective of obtaining a license that would enable me to impart my enthusiasm for dancing and instruct others on the fundamentals. However, my existence did not abruptly come to a halt in that location.

In preparation for an occasion such as this, I pursued numerous courses in the EITI, which have significantly altered my perspective on God. I dedicated myself entirely to the Kingdom Ambassador Ministry Training last year. During my first and second years, I completed the School of Prophecy, joined the Company of Prophets, investigated the Apostolic River, and participated in Pageantry. In years one and two, I experienced a profound urge to assume the role of Kingdom Spheres during my time in Prophetic Dance Teams. This occurred not once but twice.

I believe that God has informed me that the experience will differ on the second occasion; however, I will provide you with additional information about that later.

I had the extraordinary opportunity to compose two works during my tenure in the author's course at the EITI. My experience of attending church has been significantly altered by these courses. I can still vividly remember my time at that Methodist church, where I was overcome with an overpowering desire to break free. At that time, I found it exceedingly challenging to comprehend the reason for my profound yearning for something more from God. I have genuinely felt God's favor as I have progressed through the EITI process. I was fortunate enough to receive mentorship from Dr. Pamela Scott, the founder, in a mentorship group known as Acts 29. This year was a significant milestone for me, as I was ordained and licensed as a prophet in God's kingdom. I gained an understanding of the genuine essence of being aligned as opposed to solely attempting to conform. I have come to the realization that commitment is not merely a term; it is a genuine commitment that necessitates action and the completion of necessary tasks. I was privileged to assume the position of regional leader for the Northeast region of Ten Worldwide and the EITI as a school during my tenure at the EITI. This assignment moved me forward in leadership. I guess God had bigger plans than what I could see.

The Breaking

I experienced a sensation of flight, but then, all of a sudden, everything disintegrated. I went through a period in which I felt profoundly misunderstood, and, to be frank, there were individuals in the same ministry who appeared to be against me. This season was exceedingly taxing for me. I experienced a profound sense of devastation and a feeling that my self-worth had been completely shattered. I vividly remember Apostle Pamela informing me that I was indispensable to the kingdom and that I had to persevere, as my health was deteriorating. Those words are as fresh in my mind as if they were spoken yesterday.

I experienced an overwhelming sense of isolation; it was as though I was confined to a cave with respect to my comprehension of the kingdom's affairs. I continued to attend classes as if everything was great, but God began to uncover and reveal all of the struggles I was facing. Upon reaching a certain point, I experienced a profound sense of disconnection from the EITI. I resigned from all of my positions at the institution and opted to pursue my own path. In all honesty, I can assert that it was not the most advantageous course of action. I have a fond memory of Apostle Pamela calling me randomly to check in and convey her love and how much she missed me during this season. Her efforts to connect with me were genuinely meaningful to me, even when I felt estranged.

I can assume that you are under the impression that this passage is all about ascending, correct? I am aware that you may be interested in the reason I am disclosing this aspect of my journey. I am disclosing it to you because I wish for you to have a comprehensive understanding of my experience. Soaring does not always manifest as anticipated; occasionally, it manifests as valuable lessons acquired. During this period of feeling disoriented, I established a connection with a local ministry that I believed was facilitating my personal development. However, I ultimately came to the realization that it was no longer the appropriate fit. I was seated in a ministry that I had previously been involved with, but I no longer felt a sense of connection to it. I was under the impression that my misalignment was the cause of my difficulties.

The Awakening

As I continue on this voyage, I have found myself applying the valuable lessons I have learned from each experience I have had thus far. My experience with Dr. Pamela has been replete with unforgettable firsts, such as my initial flight to Jamaica. The conference we attended together was an unforgettable educational experience for me. That was only the commencement of my journey; there are still numerous additional international events that await me. During these excursions, I acquired a wealth of knowledge regarding the formation of teams and the genuine comprehension of the Apostolic flow. I was prepared to revolutionize the entire environment rather than merely becoming a performer. This was all a component of the voyage that God had specifically designed for me.

I would like to relate a personal anecdote regarding my initial encounter with the founder of the EITI. It was not the most joyous occasion for me. I was in a dance course, and I was having difficulty understanding the fundamentals. Additionally, there was an assignment that I was uninterested in completing. Following this, I received a telephone call from the class administrator informing me that Apostle Pamela desired to meet with me. As a result of that conversation, I can confidently assert that the assignment was completed, and this marked the commencement of my mentor-mentee relationship with Apostle Pamela. I am once again confident in the knowledge that God has a plan for me. I have come to the realization that my understanding of loyalty and honor has been significantly influenced by each of these minor interactions as I reflect on my voyage. I have come to accept criticism and acknowledge that not all individuals have malicious intentions; some genuinely care about my well-being. Reflecting on my experience in the EITI, I am compelled to share the valuable lessons that each error I made taught me. Ultimately, each misstep resulted in a positive outcome, which influenced my trajectory in unexpected ways.

I was extremely disheartened by the grades I received in class. Despite my awareness that these courses were intended to enhance my character, I was unable to escape the sensation that they were simultaneously undermining my self-assurance. I had consistently maintained the practice of establishing and accomplishing personal objectives. These courses demonstrated to me that I was not proficient in all areas, and they assisted me in comprehending that there was a degree of pride associated with this realization. I would like to convey that acknowledging and confronting my pride was a substantial accomplishment in my life. I came to the realization that this was a challenge that I would never have to face again as I continued to ascend. Although I was in school, I encountered numerous challenging circumstances that significantly influenced my later life. I am genuinely uncertain as to how I would have been able to complete the course without the assistance of three specific instructors at the EITI.

They were instrumental in assisting me in maintaining my composure and determining my course of action. I have come to understand the true meaning of the term "needing more." I experienced a period in my life during which I was convinced that I was deserving of recognition, and it was difficult for me to understand why I was being disregarded. I discovered myself discussing my thoughts with Dr. Kina Arnold, a teacher, in the hallway at the Summit during graduation.

Honor In Understanding:

Dr. Arnold dedicated time to converse with me, and her words added a layer of wisdom to my life. After a few years, I resolved to enroll in the course she was instructing. We established a fantastic relationship because of our previous encounter, and she continued to invest in me. I am compelled to disclose that she has played a substantial role in the voyage that God has mapped out for me, and I will elaborate on this soon.

The second individual who assisted me was Apostle Janelle, who also served as a teacher at the institution. In 2017, I encountered her at the Summit for the first time. Although our encounter was not particularly noteworthy, it appeared to be a divine intervention that brought her into my life. I was unaware that this was the beginning of my elevation and promotion, but I was presented with the opportunity to establish a prophetic team through the course she co-taught, and we formed a fantastic bond.

Apostle Pamela is the final individual I wish to acknowledge, as she was by my side for the duration of the EITI voyage. I neglected to mention that, during this period, I was not only confronted with my own health issues but was also mourning my mother's passing as she transitioned to be with the Lord. Dr. Pamela was the first person I spoke to during what I can only characterize as the most difficult experience of my life, and it was a true blessing. It is difficult to comprehend that I lost both of my parents; however, I must acknowledge that God has introduced me to another mother. I began to encounter some genuinely remarkable moments that felt like divine surprises after I had recovered from the initial shock. Do you remember the time I mentioned that God inspired me to re-enroll in the Kingdom Spheres class during a Summit session? I was unable to comprehend the reason at that time, but I opted to comply with His request. Subsequently, everything underwent a positive transformation. I was provided with a church building at no cost and was motivated to pursue a new direction during my time in the course.

Victory in the Making

The commissioning of me into the office of the Apostle was an extraordinary experience, and I have since adopted my role as a servant leader of the Heart of God Gathering Place. Do you recall the initial teacher I mentioned who entered my existence? She was the pageantry instructor, and she provided me with the guidance necessary to establish a church environment that accurately depicts the beauty of heaven for all who attend. The other teacher who was supposed to assist me in the development of a dance team was unable to fully comprehend her responsibility to help me establish a robust leadership team for the center that God ultimately entrusted to me. However, Dr. Pamela is my guiding light, and her dedication and connection to my ascent are invaluable to me. I would like to take this opportunity to express my sincere gratitude and respect for the love and support that she has consistently extended to me, even when I felt that I was undeserving of it. Through the EITI, I have been fortunate to have the support of numerous exceptional individuals. However, I must not overlook the author mentors. They were consistently present, motivating me to persevere and avoid failure. I am authentically supported by them, and they provide me with the guidance necessary to continue progressing. I am currently enrolled in a doctoral program, enthusiastically anticipating the next chapter of my life as I embrace my journey in ministry as a cycle-breaker.

As I have recounted my experience with the EITI, I trust that you will recognize the significance of each lesson I acquired in the context of my personal development. God perceived the obstacles I encountered as victories. I can observe how God has worked through each error I have made, as it has served as a stepping stone for my personal development. It was my errors that ultimately resulted in my successes! I have come to the realization that each moment offers me a distinctive opportunity to make a different decision.

ABOUT THE AUTHOR

I'm Apostle Tesha Hall—wife, mother, new grandmother, and passionate servant leader of The Heart of God Gathering Place Apostolic Hub. Called to equip Kingdom leaders, I walk boldly in my prophetic mandate, blending ministry with marketplace leadership, all while pursuing my doctoral degree and living Jeremiah 29:11 daily.

I SPOKE TO YOU: BEFORE I FORMED YOU

INTRODUCTION

Blessings, Beloved, I am Melissa Hardy, author of the book *I Spoke to You: Before I Formed You*. Have you ever asked yourself, "Who am I? or "Why am I Here?" and still feel uncertain? If so, *I Spoke to You* will connect you to the voice of Papa God—a place of intimacy and His divine plan for you. Throughout this chapter, I will share intimate parts of my journey to help you hear His voice, discover your Kingdom identity, and birth your purpose.

Before Papa God formed you, He spoke your divine purpose, callings, and giftings. And then, He placed you in your mother's womb and sent you to Earth, for His Glory! To walk out your calling—His legacy, which is a manifestation of Kingdom history—to relive what has already taken place in Heaven.

"Before I formed you (BELOVED) *in the womb I knew you [and approved of you as My chosen instrument], And before you were born, I consecrated you [to Myself as My own]; I have appointed you* (BELOVED) *as a prophet to the nations* (YOUR SPECIFIC CALLING)" (Jeremiah 1:5 AMP, alterations mine).

"That which is has already been, and that which will be has already been, for God seeks what has passed by [so that history repeats itself]" (Ecclesiastes 3:15 AMP).

God is the beginning (THE ALPHA—THE CREATOR) and the end (THE OMEGA—THE FINISHER). Therefore, everything on Earth has already been created, executed, and completed in Heaven. God longs for you to S.O.A.R. with Him—you are a conduit from Heaven to Earth, For His Glory!

Sold Out And Radical (S.O.A.R.) For HIM!

TESTIMONY

Who Am I? Why Am I Here? What Is My Calling or Purpose in Life?

I spent years searching for the answers to these questions. In 2017, I heard a message on the simplicity of uncovering my calling, purpose, and identity. The speaker simply stated that I should ask Papa God (my Creator) the following question: "What did You say to me before You made me and placed me in my mother's womb?" So, I started asking Him the question, and then early one morning I heard His audible voice, and He spoke the following (condensed version):

You are a healer to The Nations! You will deliver millions of people from the hands of the enemy. Everything you do and have been through is tied to delivering MY people.

You are MY philanthropist, a conveyer belt from heaven, and I will entrust you with millions of dollars to deliver people and to build places for them to be delivered to.

You are MY mouthpiece—you are MY prophet! Your great name will be known as MY FIRE, MY secret weapon—FIRE, FIRE, FIRE, FIRE is who you are.

Because of the mandate on your life, you must be able to see through MY lenses, to hear what I hear, to sense and feel what I do. You must live and operate from the supernatural—NO FEAR, only courage and boldness. I am the key to the revelation, power, anointing, fire, healing, prophecies, deliverance, and wealth that will flow through you. Your names are:

- Consuming Fire – Everything you touch will be consumed, transformed, and purified with MY FIRE.
- Fire Bug – You will start FIRES everywhere you go.
- Diamond – You have been through the FIRE your whole life, and it's time for you to shine.
- Glitter Fire – Refined diamonds help others through the process of purification.

At the end of my Daddy encounter, the light switch within me had been turned on. At that very moment, I knew that I knew who I was. As I walked in the freedom of my Kingdom Calling and Identity, Papa God revealed the devil's strategies, which included:

The Spirit of Infirmity – Which resulted in 42 illness claims in my military retirement disability entitlement.

The Spirit of Death – Numerous accidents, which included neck, back, traumatic brain, and jaw injuries (knocking out all my teeth).

Molestation, Spirit of Hatred, and PTSD – Physical, emotional, and verbal abuse as well as molestation, military combat, and sexual harassment manifested in depression, anxiety, and alcohol abuse.

All these assassination strategies resulted in me:

Living in a CAVE of low self-esteem, unworthiness, self-doubt, and not having a voice.

Hiding behind the MASK of PERFECTIONISM—I expected perfection in myself and others.

Living a life as a MASTER CONTROLLER—I believed that if I could control everything and everyone around me, nothing bad would or could happen.

While the strategies of the devil were extreme in my life, he had already lost the battle before it began. Before Papa God "SPOKE TO ME" and formed me and placed me in my mother's womb, I had already victoriously completed my Kingdom Calling in Heaven.

My Story and Your Story in Heaven were completed before they began on Earth.

HEARING HIS VOICE

"There is nothing more powerful, impactful, and life-changing than hearing the voice of your Creator, Papa God."

LOVE NOTE

"My Beloved, Oh how I long for times of intimacy with you—times that belong to YOU and ME only. Moments where OUR hearts are intertwined as one, and MY VOICE, MY HEARTBEAT for you is flowing freely. It's in this place of intimacy that you will fully know how much I desire to be in YOUR presence and how much I love you.

I love You, Papa God."

Hearing God's voice may not be something you experience on a normal basis. The key to hearing the Voice of God is that it requires you to enter His presence. It is in these intimate encounters that God reveals His Heart toward you.

You can experience God encounters through times of fasting, praying, worshipping, soaking, prophetic activations, journaling, and reflecting (Selah) in His presence. Encountering God comes from a deep desire to want to know Him more. This only happens when you spend time with Him, setting aside time to actively listen to what He is saying.

My Story: *After I received salvation at the age of 23, it took me years to learn how to hear the voice of Papa God for myself. Learning to hear His voice required a relationship, and back then, I didn't view God as Papa God. He was God—the one who disciplined me when I made mistakes or sinned. My view was based on my dysfunctional relationship with my natural father.*

My inability to see God as a loving father resulted in me becoming codependent on others to hear for me. This codependency fueled my weakness for wanting to please people. As a people pleaser, I allowed others to hear from God for me and to guide my decision-making process. During these years, I made a lot of bad decisions, which severely impacted my immediate family members and others. During my Christian Counseling and attending Bible College, I slowly uncovered the root of codependency, and Papa God healed this area of my life.

And as I healed, God became My Papa God—My Father—and I began chasing after Him as a little girl runs after her Daddy. And as I pursued Him through prayer, worship, and reading His Word, our relationship began to blossom. I would find myself in His presence, and He would begin to communicate with me through visions, through dreams, and audibly. During our times of intimacy, Papa God would share His heart toward me, and He would tell me how much He loved me. I love being in His presence so much … I became a chaser of His presence … and then I transitioned to living from His presence.

KINGDOM IDENTITY

"Before God created you, He had already predetermined every unique detail about you, Beloved."

LOVE NOTE

"My Beloved, I am the Master Creator; it is only I who can define you. There is no need to look beyond ME, for I hold the answers to all your questions. Anything or anyone outside of ME will result in a counterfeit response to all your questions relating to your calling, giftings, purpose, identity, and true authenticity. The simplicity in the answers you're searching for simply lies in asking ME this very simple question: 'Papa God, what did YOU say to me before YOU formed me and placed me in my mother's womb?' There are so many things I SPOKE TO YOU, Before Your Time on Earth. Come and hear MY Voice, My Beloved, as I reveal the REAL YOU!

Oh, how I love You, Papa God."

Think about how much time God took to imagine everything visible and invisible to mankind. It is beyond your capacity to know and understand the magnitude of God's process of **IMAGINATION** and His **CREATIVE** power. There is only one way to unlock the mysteries of creation, and that is through an intimate relationship with Him so that you can hear His heart and voice for your life.

Before God CREATED you, He IMAGINED everything about you—your purpose, calling, assignments, gifts and talents, and the color of your hair and eyes. God even numbered the hairs of your head: *"Indeed the very hairs of your head are all numbered ..."* (Luke 12:7 AMP, alterations mine).

And then GOD SPOKE TO YOU all the things HE had imagined about you—and then He FORMED you and PLACED you in your mother's womb. In the Book of Psalms, King David wrote, *"For You formed my innermost parts; you knit me [together] in my mother's womb. I will give thanks and praise to You, for I am fearfully and wonderfully made; Wonderful are Your works, and my soul knows it very well"* (Psalm 139:13-14, AMP).

> *My Story: I spent 52 years searching for my identity ... I looked at others for validation ... I tried to define myself as an Army Soldier ... I claimed leadership titles and positions ... I served in numerous church ministries. At the end of each day, I found myself standing in the dark—lost and empty. But one day, I heard the very words PAPA GOD SPOKE TO ME before HE CREATED ME, and suddenly, I found myself standing in the light. There are no words to describe that very moment in time.*

ACTIVATION

The Unveiling of Your "God Spoke to You" Moment

The time has come to hear the very words GOD SPOKE TO YOU before HE CREATED YOU—He has been waiting on you. Ask Him the following question with an expectation to hear His voice: "Daddy, what did You say to me before You formed me and placed me in my mother's womb?" Once you've heard from Daddy, it is imperative for you to journal His spoken words.

Your monumental moment can be overwhelming and beyond anything you could ever have imagined. Take time to bask in His presence and your newly discovered identity. You may need to spend time meditating on His life-changing words or entering a time of fasting, prayer, and worship. During your time of intimacy, He may reveal that you need to enter a time of healing before giving birth to your calling.

You cannot BIRTH Heaven to Earth if you are carrying brokenness and unforgiveness. Entering the BIRTHING ROOM without healing these wounds is life-threatening to your calling (baby)—and may result in hindering the birthing process (becoming stuck), abortion (death of your calling), or a premature birth (being born too early). This is a very critical time in your life. I pray you surrender and meet Papa God in the operating room prior to moving forward.

SURVIVING THE BIRTHING ROOM

"You were made to BIRTH HEAVEN to Earth."

LOVE NOTE

"My Beloved, the birthing process can be quite painful, and you will encounter many trials, attacks, and challenges. Why? Because the devil does not want you to birth your destiny. He will do anything to stop you from BIRTHING HEAVEN on Earth. You are in the fight of your life—stay focused on ME and know that you have already won and are soaring with ME.

I love you, Papa God."

Keys to surviving the BIRTHING ROOM:
- Move under God's timing and not yours or someone else's.
- Keep your eyes on Him and not on the trials and challenges.
- Stay rooted in the Word.
- Stay in His Presence—through worship.
- Decree, Declare, and Proclaim His promises.
- Don't take unauthorized people into the Birthing Room.
- Live from the Throne Room—it is already finished.
- Walk in your Power and Authority!

I want to share my story, not to scare or to discourage you from entering the birthing room, but to encourage you that Papa God has prepared you and is with you in the birthing room.

While I was writing "I SPOKE TO YOU," there were several times when Papa God required me to return to the operating room to deal with areas of brokenness that were hindering my birthing process. I found myself stuck—unable to move forward!

Through my willingness to return to the operating room, I was able to SOAR and birth "I SPOKE TO YOU."

My Story – From the moment I said yes to birth "I SPOKE TO YOU: Before I Formed You," I battled and overcame great personal challenges:

- *I had allergic bronchial asthma, sinus infections, and COVID.*
- *I experienced carpal tunnel, golfer's elbow, and shoulder pain— so severe I could not write or type.*
- *Several family members battled with suicidal tendencies.*
- *The devil constantly questioned my calling and identity, which resulted in writer's block.*
- *I was subjected to a hostile work environment.*
- *My husband underwent his fifth liver cancer surgery.*

Papa God would never have placed a calling within you and me if we were not able to withstand, bear, tolerate, and endure the birthing room process so that we can S.O.A.R. with HIM.

ACTIVATION

"My Beloved, Oh, how I have waited for this moment in time. Come and take My hand, let us enter the birthing room together.

I love you, Papa God."

Release and surrender your heart through WORSHIP, and enter the birthing room with great expectation. I can see your baby leaping in your womb and beginning to push with great force and strength—can you feel your baby leaping and pushing?

"It is time to birth the very words Papa God spoke over you before time."

I highly encourage you to read the entire book *I SPOKE TO YOU: BEFORE I FORMED YOU*, which can be purchased on Amazon or at i.spoke.to.you.beloved@gmail.com. The book will take you through a process of:

- Learning you have been called for such a time as NOW!
- Understanding your Kingdom identity.
- Cultivating your relationship with Papa God.
- Legacy building.

COME FORTH, BUTTERFLY, AND SOAR!

ABOUT THE AUTHOR

Melissa Hardy is passionately devoted to helping people embrace their God-given identities and destinies. She is a Fire Branded Prophet and Healer to the Nations who carries the FIRE of Revival for the End Times. She is called to equip the Body of Christ for the advancement of the Kingdom.

FROM THE DANCE TO THE NATIONS

Legacy in Motion: The Early Stirring

"Though your beginning was small, yet your latter end would increase abundantly" (Job 8:7 NKJV).

Let this remind you that no start is too insignificant when God writes your story. Growth is inevitable when you walk in divine purpose.

From my earliest days growing up on the twin-island nation of Trinidad and Tobago, I now realize that the hand of God has always been upon me. What looked like simple childhood play—standing on my grandmother's feet as she moved gracefully, teaching me how to dance—was actually divine training. She was the first person to recognize the gift within me, and she nurtured it without even knowing the full extent of where it would lead.

"Train up a child in the way he should go, and when he is old he will not depart from it" (Proverbs 22:6 NKJV).

What began as innocent joy became the foundation of my calling. Dance was never just movement for me; it was ministry, a prophetic expression of my spirit's cry to worship God.

My First Yes: Called to Dance

"But they that wait upon the Lord shall renew their strength; they shall mount up with wings as eagles ..." (Isaiah 40:31 KJV).

Endurance, strength, and divine timing—a perfect image for rising from grief into purpose.

In 2011, I took a major step of faith by enrolling in the Eagles International Training Institute's (EITI's) Dance Year 1 program. That decision changed my life forever. Though I couldn't attend the graduation ceremony in Dallas, Texas, due to a necessary back surgery, I knew something powerful had been activated in me. Sometimes, God allows stillness to prepare us for soaring.

By 2012, I was finally able to attend my first Gathering of the Eagles Summit. That trip was more than a milestone—it was a divine appointment. I stayed at the home of Apostle Pamela Scott, and in those few days, God began to do a deep work in me. Her home was a place of peace, and her presence a prophetic signal of what God was doing in my life.

But while I was there, I received a painful phone call from Trinidad: My grandmother, the very one who first taught me to dance, had fallen ill and was being rushed to the hospital. Early the next morning, I learned she had passed.

I was devastated. I wept. I questioned God. But in that moment of sorrow, He spoke so clearly to me. He reminded me that my grandmother had been the one to first train me and affirm my gift. And now, He was passing the baton to Apostle Pamela—my new teacher. It was as though one generation was releasing me to the next.

That moment marked me deeply. I could feel the weight of a new mantle falling on me. God was calling me to soar!

The Room Was Too Small

After graduating as an Eagle, I knew God had not only equipped me—He had entrusted me with a call to build spaces where others could worship and grow. One of those spaces was Dance-A-Rama, an annual gathering I hosted that brought together dance ministries from local churches for a night of extravagant praise before the Lord.

What began with a few faithful groups soon expanded into a regional movement. Ministries from different islands and backgrounds showed up, year after year, ready to pour out their worship in movement. Dance-A-Rama wasn't just an event; it became a spiritual altar—a place where Heaven touched Earth through prophetic dance.

At the final Dance-A-Rama I led in 2014, something unforgettable happened. A visiting Eagle from Puerto Rico shared a vision God had shown her during the service. In that vision, she saw me standing in a building, but my head was above the roof, and my arms were extended out both windows. Her words were clear:

"The place you're in is too small."

She had no idea that just prior to that event, I had been in deep prayer, asking God for direction. I was feeling depleted—pouring out consistently, yet not feeling replenished. That prophetic word hit my spirit like a lightning bolt. It was confirmation, but it also raised new questions. What next? Where do I go from here?

For two years, I waited.

No doors. No clarity. Just silence ... and trust.

Then, God did something unexpected. He sent me to a church that was considerably smaller than the one I had just outgrown. I honestly laughed and said, "So much for the last place being too small!" But God, in His infinite wisdom and sense of humor, was setting me up for something bigger than space—He was setting me up for alignment.

At that ministry, I met a powerful woman of God who is now deceased. Her leadership, mentorship, and trust helped launch me into a new season. She gave me room to spread my wings—to lead, preach, build, and shape the apostolic culture of the house. What looked smaller in the natural was actually larger in impact. I wasn't just ministering—I was being developed, challenged, and released.

That's when I truly began to mount up.

God used that seemingly small place to stretch me, sharpen me, and prepare me to soar. Looking back, Dance-A-Rama was a seed—but what came after was the harvest.

The Mantle Falls: From Grief to Glory

As I sat under the ministry of the EITI and the mentorship of powerful leaders like Apostle Pamela, my eyes were opened to a bigger picture. God wasn't just calling me to dance; He was calling me to soar like the eagle—to go beyond my territory, beyond my comfort zone, beyond perceived limitations. An eagle doesn't fear the storm; it uses the winds to ascend. Through my alignment with the EITI, God expanded my vision. The wings of my purpose stretched far beyond choreography and movement. He gave me a new lens to see the needs of my nation and the Caribbean region. There was a hunger for leadership, a thirst for sound doctrine, and a desperate cry for apostolic training. There were so many hungry, gifted people waiting for someone to help unlock what was inside of them.

> *"But they that wait upon the Lord shall renew their strength; they shall mount up with wings as eagles ..."*
> (Isaiah 40:31 KJV).

Through the tools I received from the EITI, I launched into new territory. I began teaching leadership courses and equipping Kingdom ambassadors in the British Virgin Islands. The more I poured out, the more God poured in.

Over the past twelve years, I've hosted countless conferences and workshops that have brought together people from across the Caribbean and even beyond. I've witnessed God heal, restore, and rejuvenate His people in powerful ways. Children have been blessed, the elderly have been supported, and ministries have been revived—all through simple obedience.

> *"Enlarge the place of your tent, stretch your tent curtains wide, do not hold back ..."* (Isaiah 54:2 NIV).

I didn't realize it at first, but God had placed a gathering anointing on my life. He gave me the grace to unite leaders, worshippers, and ministers from various walks of life into spaces of refreshing and revival. I wasn't just planning events—I was stewarding atmospheres where Heaven could touch Earth.

From Student to Apostle: The EITI and the Send

> *"Ask of me, and I will give you the nations as your inheritance, and the ends of the earth as your possession"* (Psalm 2:8 NKJV).

The apostolic call to global impact—a divine promise that what you ask in obedience, He will entrust to your stewardship.

In October 2016, I was officially commissioned and ordained as an Apostle through the Eagles International Training Institute. I knew then that my life would never be the same. It wasn't just a title; it was a commissioning to go deeper, to dig wells, and to build for the Kingdom.

> *"And He gave some, apostles; and some, prophets; and some, evangelists; and some, pastors and teachers ..."* (Ephesians 4:11 KJV).

Since that moment, I have leaned fully into the call. I launched the Kingdom Ambassador Ministerial Training Program in the

British Virgin Islands, and I've had the honor of mentoring many leaders—men and women who are now walking confidently in their assignments.

God has given me the joy of leading both the EITI and The Eagles Network (TEN) in my country, where over sixty people have successfully graduated from the TEN program across Tortola and Virgin Gorda. Seeing their growth has been one of the greatest rewards of my journey.

Later, I was appointed as the international director of TEN, overseeing all English-speaking nations where TEN operates. Only God could have orchestrated that—taking a girl who once stood on her grandmother's feet to learn how to dance and raising her up to speak into nations.

Marketplace Mandate: Apostolic Excellence Beyond the Pulpit

One of the greatest lessons I've learned is that the Kingdom of God is not confined to the four walls of a church. As much as I minister in sanctuaries, I am also called to be a light in the marketplace.

For years, I've served in the banking industry—a world that many wouldn't immediately associate with ministry. Yet, I've come to see the marketplace as one of the greatest mission fields. What began as a role in customer service evolved into a divine assignment to lead with integrity, discernment, and compassion.

For the past six years, I have served as the branch manager at a local bank. It has been a journey of stretching, growth, and refining. Managing a team and overseeing the branch operations of a financial institution has required more than business acumen—it has demanded wisdom, patience, and the heart of a servant.

Whether managing financial solutions, leading my team, or making executive decisions, I've come to recognize that I carry apostolic grace—even in a blazer and heels. Ministry doesn't pause when I leave the pulpit. It walks with me into meetings and every customer interaction.

That same grace to lead and multiply began to overflow into my own ventures. As I matured in the marketplace, God began to birth dreams within me that extended beyond the corporate world. I wasn't just called to support someone else's vision—I was also called to build.

With my family, I launched The Circle Café, and our motto is "When you're here, you're family." This cozy, family-centered restaurant quickly became more than just a place to eat. It's a gathering spot where food and family meet—a space where conversations about purpose, family, and hope happen over shared meals. From our kitchen to the community, we serve more than just physical nourishment; we serve joy, connection, and comfort.

In addition to the restaurant, we launched Suits You, a boutique designed to empower working women through fashion rooted in faith. It's not just about clothes—it's about confidence. Every suit, every piece is chosen with intention, helping women walk into their assignments with boldness and style.

These ventures represent the heart of who I am—a woman committed to building platforms that reflect the Kingdom, no matter the setting. Whether behind a desk, at the altar, or in a business meeting, I know I'm called to create, to steward, and to lead with excellence.

Adonai Dance Garments and Accessories was also birthed to create custom garments and worship tools for dance ministers throughout the islands. This business is not just creative—it's prophetic. Dressing worshippers for their assignments is an act of honor.

> *"Whatever you do, work heartily, as for the Lord and not for men"* (Colossians 3:23 ESV).

Discipled, Trained, and Released

In 2019, the Lord impressed upon Dr. Pamela Scott the importance of teams in this new era of ministry. She declared, "The blessing is in the cluster," anchoring this revelation in Isaiah 65:8 (NKJV): *"As the new wine is found in the cluster ... so will I do for My servants' sake."* This powerful insight birthed the Prophetic Dance Teams initiative, a training designed to shift dance ministry from solo expression to corporate prophetic movement. Over the years, Apostle Diane Peters from Anguilla and I have had the honor of co-teaching this course. Together, we continue to impart the fundamentals of building and sustaining effective prophetic dance teams—equipping leaders with practical tools, spiritual insight, and the apostolic covering needed to build their prophetic dance ministry.

In March 2024, I officially launched the REACH Apostolic Training Center—a space dedicated to equipping and commissioning Kingdom leaders for global impact. What began as a vision in prayer became a hub for development, sharpening, and sending. In this season, God also divinely aligned me with Apostle Tesha Hall and *The Heart of God Gathering Place*. Though we are in different nations, God reminded me that He is still building apostolic teams across borders. Together, we've been able to partner through my Monday night online training sessions, creating a space for ongoing discipleship and leadership growth. We also launched a Wednesday night Apostolic Surge, where teaching and activation flow freely across time zones. It's a testament to how God's plans transcend geography—and how divine alignment can accelerate Kingdom purpose.

Still Soaring: My Ongoing Yes

Looking back, I can say without hesitation that I am who I am by the grace of God—and I am a by-product of the great work being done through the Eagles International Training Institute.

The EITI was not just a program for me. It was family. It was alignment. It was the launching pad for my destiny.

To every dancer who feels like they're just "performing," I want to say—your movement matters.

To every woman who's balancing ministry, business, and family—there is strength and wisdom available to you.

To every emerging leader who feels overlooked—God sees you, and He's preparing you for the nations.

My story is proof that when you surrender your gifts to God, He will breathe on them and take you further than you ever dreamed.

"But as it is written: 'Eye has not seen, nor ear heard, nor have entered into the heart of man the things which God has prepared for those who love Him'" (1 Corinthians 2:9 NKJV).

I am still soaring, still serving, and still saying yes. And I will keep flying, as long as the wind of the Spirit lifts these wings.

What gift has God placed in you that may seem small now, but—if surrendered fully—could impact nations for His glory? Are you willing to let Him take you from where you started to where He's calling you to soar?

ABOUT THE AUTHOR

Apostle Janelle L. Jagdeo, originally from Trinidad and Tobago, is a dynamic leader, dance minister, and entrepreneur in the British Virgin Islands. She founded Adonai Arts Academy and REACH Apostolic Training Center, is an EITI and TEN nation leader, manages multiple businesses, and is passionate about empowering others through ministry and the arts.

THE DOOR AND THE FLAME: A REFLECTION OF SURRENDER AND RESTORATION

Introduction

Shhhhh … Both ancient and holy, rhythmically pursuing through the corridors of eternity. Shhhhh … There it goes again, rhapsody meeting renaissance; grace dripping with glory. Shhhhh … It is the sound of mercy penetrating a door long shut, a cry of love calling, calling, calling out to the one who thought they were too far gone.

My friend, this is more than the beginning of a journey. In fact, it is the stirring of a soul. My soul, your soul, our soul. It is the summoning of a soul to be wrapped in a flame, whispered with tenderness back to life. It is the beckoning of the weary, the hidden, the hardened … It is the sound of His nearness.

He knocks. He knocks. And still, He yet knocks again.

And if you dare to open, only if you dare, not only will you see HIM …

You will soon see *YOU*.

The *YOU* that HE has always known, the *YOU* that HE is longing for.

So, come.

The journey awaits, but the knocking will not last forever …

Preface: The One Who Waits

This rhythmical journey begins with a knocking—one that is slow and steady, void of the urgency of a frantic foe, but resembling that of an endearing love.

His arrival, the moment I am awaiting, etched in the fabric of eternity. What will it be like, and what will He do? It happens, and when it does, He stands at the door—not as a stranger, but One who is quite familiar with this place. His approach is as though He has visited here many times before as one who has committed this delivery stop to memory. He stands, not as one who is disgruntled by this assignment, but as the One who fashioned my very soul. Standing still, with fire in His eyes and mercy in His scars, He waits. He waits, and then, He knocks. His knock is not one of force but one distinct of a divine pursuit.

What you are holding in your hands is not merely a collection of beautifully penned words; nor is it a meager attempt to draw your pity. Oh no, my dear one, it is far more than that. It is the journey of a cry, one that pierces the very depth of the human soul. It is an amber alert that shakes the heavens and forces creation to take a step back, all while beckoning it to its place of purpose. What you are holding in your hands is a call …

A call into the quiet places,

Into the wrestling,

Into the burning,

Into the beauty.

A call into the loving arms of the One who sees no wrongdoing and longs to be with you, with me, with us.

What you are holding was written for the one who has closed the door.

The one who has sat in silence.

The one who thinks they've gone too far.

The one who has seen enough, heard enough, and had enough.

It's for the one who hears the knock but doesn't want to open.

The one, just like you, just like me, just like us.

This is a journey. A movement.

Etched in the wounds of the One who would stop at nothing to hold you close again.

This is a journey. A movement.

Through surrender.

Through fire.

This is a journey. A movement.

Through the echo of the One who never stopped calling your name.

Can you hear Him? He's calling you; He's calling your name.

I challenge you to believe that, just this once, if you're brave enough to open the door, you won't just meet Him.

You'll find yourself, too. The YOU that you thought would be lost forever.

You'll find yourself. The YOU He always knew.

You'll find yourself. The YOU that you so desperately wanted never to forgive, wanted to forget.

That you. The YOU that He loves.

You'll find yourself, just like I did.

So come, come with me, and I promise, I'll hold your hand as we go through this journey together. And if you're willing, only if you are willing, you will find yourself again.

But before we begin, I ask only one thing. That you will listen. Just listen.

Are you ready? Come on.

Wait, wait a minute, do you hear that?

Listen closely.

He knocks.

Movement I: The Knock
(The Beginning: The Sound That Stirred My Soul)

There is a sound. Do you hear it? There it goes again.

No, not loud at all; not thundering nor demanding. But a sound, nonetheless.

Just a knock, ancient and eternal, yet persistent and powerful.

It does not rush. Oh no …

It does not rage. Oh no …

It waits. Oh yes, it waits …

The sound, that sound, is the sound of compassion combined with rhythm. The beating on a cymbal; the striking of a snare. It beats.

A knock of grace wrapped in patience. Covered with the tenderest of mercies.

It echoes through the chambers of time, reverberating through the cracks in my soul.

A knocking that knows my name and one that will know yours, too, if you let it.

It's so powerful that even when you've forgotten it, it doesn't forget you.

"Behold, I stand at the door and knock …"

(Revelation 3:20 KJV)

Even now, there it goes again.

Not once. Not twice.

But again. And again. A continuous cadence of rhapsody eclipsing upon the chambers of my heart. It's painstakingly beautiful as I try my best to hide from it all. Fear, torment, shame. They should be able to drown out the knocking, they should. But …

Still … He knocks.

Reflection: Movement I
(The Echo Remains)

Beloved soul, pause.

In the stillness of the moment, pause …

Let His knocking settle you amid the silence.

Let it find its way into the hollowed parts of your heart and the shallow places in your soul.

Let it echo.

You've heard it, haven't you? You've heard it to the point where you refused to listen anymore.

Maybe you heard it …

In the quiet of night …

In the anguish of your laughter.

In the place you swore you would never go again.

Yet still …

He knocks.

Let your heart speak and your pen respond.

- Where do you hear the knock?
- What name does He call you when He knocks?
- What would it take to open the door—not tomorrow, but now?

A Whispered Response

(*Write your own or begin with this.*)

Come, come, He who knocks on the door of my soul,

Tap to the rhythms I so desperately tried to forget.

Dismantle the silence I called safety; destroy the pillars I called strength.

No, I am far from ready, but I am listening.

Knock again, I ask; knock again.

And I will try to answer.

Movement II: The Silence (The Resistance: Where My Soul Hides)

I heard the knock. Startling. Deafening. Unbearable in the place called shame. I tried to suffocate the sounds of agony by forcing my tears to trade places, and yet, its tremors came near.

I muffled my cries and tried to stay silent. Not because I didn't recognize the sound; on the contrary, it was a melody that I had studied far too well and much too long. It was a sound that I had welcomed many times before and now, it was a sound that I wanted so hard to forget. Yes, I must admit that I recognized the sound, and it terrified me.

So, I stayed quiet. Still. Stone-like. Ignoring it like the ringing of a doorbell early on Sunday morning.

I made my silence a sanctuary, a place of solitary confinement. A place where I could hide from healing and pretend I didn't need it. It would be better for Him to just leave, I would say to myself. Trying to believe that He would be better off without me—one less problem to try to solve.

But still, He stayed. Waiting. Whispering. Never walking away.

"I have loved you with an everlasting love..."

(Jeremiah 31:3 NKJV)

The words pierced like a physician's scalpel, tearing right through the walled chambers within my chest. I could not breathe; gasping for air, I clutched at my heart, mind swirling in sheer confusion. Desperate for it all to end, I felt myself crumbling, Crashing. Colliding with condemnation. I couldn't bear it any longer, I wanted it all to end. Just end.

I wept in silence. And that was enough for Him to stay. Waiting. For me to let Him in.

Reflection: Movement II (When Silence Becomes Your Sanctuary)

You knew the sound; you couldn't escape it.

You'd known it for years and simply couldn't shake it.

But shame taught you just how to hide,

and silence became your sword and shield.

Now, in this moment ...

What is your silence saying? And what is your silence asking?

Let your heart speak what your lips cannot.

- What have you been hiding from Him?

- When did silence become safer than surrender?
- What do you hear when everything else goes quiet?

**Write a whisper. Or a weeping.
He will hear them both.**

I hoped You would stop knocking,

but You didn't.

I wished You wouldn't stay,

but You did.

I thought my silence would protect me,

but it only kept me from Your healing.

I thought if I ignored long enough,

You would turn away.

Still ... You wait.

I am here now. Even if trembling.

I am here now.

Movement III: The Creaking Door (The Yielding: The First Movement of Surrender)

Suddenly, the silence was interrupted with a long, slow drawl. Movement on the other side of the wall that I had built to keep Him out.

It didn't burst open like I hoped nor swing wide like in stories filled with rage, slamming against the wall, causing the door pane to shake. Nor did it swing wide like freedom on the last day of school.

Instead, the door hesitated, or was it He that hesitated?

No, it didn't swing open like I thought it would. But instead …

It creaked.

Like bones remembering how to move.

It creaked.

Like trust trying to live again.

It creaked.

Like a love that knows no bounds.

It creaked.

He looked at me, but I hid my face from Him. Unbearable. I dared not look into His eyes for fear that I would never be able to return from the place called there. I wanted to be there; I needed to be there; I deserved to be there. But He looked at me.

Not like I was broken, but just like I thought He would. Like I was His.

I didn't deserve it at all. My wrongdoings were enough for my banishment, being sentenced to a life without Him. He didn't deserve the pain that I had caused. I deserved to be cast out, admonished to bearing a scarlet letter upon my chest. And yet, He looked at me.

"Come to me, all you who are weary …"

(Matthew 11:28 NIV)

And in that sacred sliver of yes, He stepped closer. Not rushing in. Tenderly. Lovingly.

Just … present.

I didn't want to speak. I didn't need to speak. And He didn't force me to say a word.

My silence became my surrender.

Reflection: Movement III (When the Door Creaks Open)

It didn't swing wide; nor did it sway.

It simply creaked.

Like a prayer once prayed, no longer knowing its way to your lips.

Like a soul once wounded, remembering how to trust again.

It simply creaked.

Let this moment be the sound of your surrender.

Let the door of your heart speak and swing open wide.

- What does it feel like to be looked at with love instead of judgment?
- What's waiting on the other side of your creaking door?

Write what you feel, not what you think you're supposed to feel.

You didn't rush in or overwhelm me.

You waited.

You didn't overpower me or judge me.

You waited.

You waited for the "yes"

hidden in my silence,

buried in my prayer,

covered by my tears.

I have no words to give,

nothing left to say,

but I think I'm ready to be seen.

Movement IV: The Flame (The Encounter: Where Love Burns Everything but You)

He stepped in with fire. The heat was paralyzing, and yet, it seemed soothing. How? And why? Why not make this easy for us both and just do away with me? And yet, He stepped in.

Not to destroy, but to make dead things breathe again. His love penetrated every part of me, resuscitating that which was dead; revealing that which deserved to live.

The flame kissed the edges of my soul and burned off what I was never meant to carry.

"Is not My word like fire …?"
(Jeremiah 23:29 NASB)

The shame.

The striving.

The fear.

Gone.

The pride.

The indifference.

The unforgiveness.

Gone.

I didn't disappear in the fire.

I became.

Reflection: Movement IV (When the Flame Finds You)

His presence was never meant to destroy.

His presence was to burn it all away.

To burn away everything

you were never meant to carry.

Let His flame search you. Let His flame reveal to you what must go.

Ask yourself in stillness:

- What is the fire burning away in me?
- What am I still holding that was never mine to keep?
- What might I become if I let it all go?

Write about your burning and your becoming.

Fire of Your Love,

Burn away what is false.

Keep what is holy.

Make me whole in the heat of Your fiery mercy.

Movement V: The Ashes
(The Aftermath: Where Death Meets Resurrection)

What once defined me now lay in smoke.

I should have felt afraid, but I felt clean.

The ache wasn't empty anymore. The dread no longer anchored me in despair.

Even the ashes sang something sacred.

He sat with me in the wreckage. Not in disappointment, but in sheer delight.

He stared at me cloaked in ashes. Not with judgment, but with justice having its way.

> *"Build the old waste places…"*
> (Isaiah 61:4 KJV)

"From this, I will build again."

"From this, I will make beauty."

Reflection: Movement V
(When Ashes Sing)

There they lie, the things that once defined you.

There they lie, what you held as nearest and dearest.

There they are …

lying quiet and undone, unrecognizable

but even the ashes carry a song.

Let the wreckage become your witness. Let the smoldering release a new song.

Let these questions arise from the smoke:
- What died in the flame? And what lived?
- Can you believe He is not disappointed by your ashes?
- What beauty could rise from here?

Write a resurrection song. Of hope. Of promise.

You sit with me in the smoke.

You look at me with eyes of love.

You're not ashamed to call me by name.

You don't turn or run away.

You sit with me in the ruins, and yet,

You call it holy ground.

From this …

You will build again.

Movement VI: The Voice (The Restoration: Where He Calls You by Your True Name)

Then He spoke.

Not to my failure, but to my future.

Not to my sin, but to my soul.

"You are not your past."

"You are not what they did to you."

"You are not what you have come out of."

"You are Mine."

His voice became the breath in my lungs.

His whisper shaped my identity.

His delight created within me a home.

> *"This is My beloved, in whom I am well pleased."*
> (Matthew 3:17 AMP)

I was not just forgiven.

I was also named.

Reflection: Movement VI (When the Voice Names You)

His voice echoed in your soul.

He spoke to your silence

and everything changed.

The shame you heard no longer roared.

The regret you bore no longer held its power.

The aching soul now made way for His glory.

Now pause.

Let His voice reverberate in your silence.

Let this moment be sacred. Let your heart answer His call.

- What has His voice been whispering to your soul that you have been too afraid to believe?
- When you hear *"You are Mine,"* what do you feel? What do you hope?
- If He calls you *beloved*, will you dare to answer?

Write it down. Let Him rename you.

Speak, Mighty Voice of Fire—

Call me repeatedly.

Name me in the ashes.

Call me from the dust.

Sing over me in the stillness; serenade me in the silence.

I hear You.

I am listening.

I am Yours.

Movement VII: The Echo (The Becoming: Where Your Life Becomes His Voice)

I once resisted the knock. Avoided it with all my might.

Now I have succumbed to it. I now have become one.

I knock on the hearts of others with gentleness.

I carry the flame, not to consume or condemn.

But to light the way.

> *"Here I am, Lord, send me."*
> (Isaiah 6:8 NLT)

Now, I am the echo.

Of the knock.

Of the flame.

Of the Voice.

And forever now, may my life whisper:

"Come in."

Reflection: Movement VII (When You Become the Echo)

You once ran from the sound of the knock.

You cowered from the heat of the flames.

Now, you return with fire in your hands and love in your eyes.

You once hid from the thoughts of a plaguing past.

You shivered at the thought of someone knowing.

Now, you burn with holy gentleness and glow with tender righteousness.

You are no longer the one who heard. You are now the one who echoes in delight.

Let this be your sending. Let your soul light the way.

- Who in your life needs the knock you once ignored?
- How can your presence become a whisper of mercy?
- What does it mean to *carry the flame* with love, not judgment?
- What does your echo sound like?

Write a declaration. A prayer. A promise.

Now, I carry the flame.

Now, I become the voice.

I will go. Yes.

I will knock. Yes.

And with every breath,

I will say:

"Come in."

Epilogue: The Open Door (The Stillness: Where All Things Are Made New)

The journey didn't end with the flame.

It didn't end with the ashes.

It didn't end with the echo.

It ended here at an open door and with a heart no longer afraid.

There's something holy about a door that stays open.

It means I no longer live in fear of what comes in or of what might leave.

It means I trust the One who stands at the threshold. It means that I am finally free.

He doesn't knock anymore.

Not because He's gone, but because He's found a home.

Here.

With me.

The silence that once screamed with shame now hums with such peace.

The same walls that kept Him out now hold His presence in.

And I? Oh …

I no longer hide.

I no longer run.

I no longer question if I'm worthy of love like this.

I no longer walk in shame.

Because love never asked for worth.

It only asked for yes.

So if you ever wonder, wonder

If He's still knocking,

If He still comes close,

If He still calls your name in the quiet.

Let this truth hold you:

He never stopped.

And He will never stop.

And now, as I sit in the warmth of what remains,

I wait, too.

Not with fear, but with fire.

In case someone else hears the knock.

In case someone else cracks the door.

I'll be here, to whisper back the words that changed my life:

"He's good. You can open it."

"He won't leave."

"Come in."

Epilogue Prayer: Let the Flame Speak

Lord, You are my God

You are the One who knocks

Even when we run.

You are the One who knocks

Even when we hide.

You are the One who knocks

Even when we no longer believe we are worth loving.

And still, You knock.

Today, I open the door.

Not because I am ready,

But because You are worthy.

Today, I open the door.

Not because I am deserving,

But because You are my destiny.

Come in; consume me.

Cleanse me.

Call me by name again.

Burn away what I was never meant to carry.

Speak life into the silence I've lived in.

Let my ashes rise like incense, a testimony of what only grace can do.

Make me an echo of Your love.

A song of the very passion of Your heart.

A flame that guides others home.

A voice that whispers, "You are still wanted."

Here I am, Lord

Come in.

Come in.

Come in.

Amen

ABOUT THE AUTHOR

Leslyn A. Johnson is an international speaker, master life coach, and ordained five-fold minister whose passion for life centers around prayer and people! She is the founder and CEO of Leslyn A. Johnson Global, a conglomerate of organizations focused on empowering others to pursue their God-given purpose with faith.

THE WONDER OF AN EAGLE'S GROWTH

Have you ever experienced rapid seasons of sudden growth? The writer of the book of proverbs states, *"There are three things that are too amazing for me, four that I do not understand: the way of an eagle in the sky, the way of a snake on a rock, the way of a ship on the high seas, and the way of a man with a young woman"* (Proverbs 30:18-19 NIV). In this chapter I will be focusing on the eagle both naturally and spiritually and, more specifically, the growth of an eagle.

Bald eagles are documented as the fastest-growing bird in North America! Within three months, an eaglet will be bigger than its parents, with a wingspan of 6½ to 8 feet! And like that of the bird, my growth in my Kingdom identity and purpose has been one of rapid and accelerated growth since becoming a part of the Eagles International Training Institute, which for the remainder of this chapter will be referred to as the EITI. When I first I joined the EITI, I couldn't fathom how much deeper my relationship with the Lord would get or how much higher I would go to fulfill my Kingdom assignment and purpose on

Earth. Now, how do eagles grow so rapidly? According to Gary Bortolotti, a world-renowned avian biologist, bald eagles might gain more weight per day than any other north American bird. This rapid weight growth is fueled by their nutrient-rich diet of meat. I can truly say that the biblically rich word "meat" that I have been and continue to be fed with within the EITI has not only increased my knowledge of the word of God; my faith has grown exponentially as well. The word of God says in Hebrews 5:13-14 (NIV), *"Anyone who lives on milk, being still an infant, is not acquainted with the teaching about righteousness. But solid food is for the mature, who by constant use have trained themselves to distinguish good from evil."*

Beaks, Feet, & The Power of Words

Another amazing fact about the growth of an eagle is that the beak and the feet grow faster than other body parts because they are essential tools for survival and take several weeks to be fully developed. Just like an eagle, our mouths and feet are critical in living a Kingdom lifestyle and surviving the attacks of the enemy. As we are reborn into the body of Christ and grow and mature, the importance of words and what we speak becomes more and more evident. James 3:5-6 (NIV) says, *"Likewise, the tongue is a small part of the body, but it makes great boasts. Consider what a great forest is set on fire by a small spark."* Proverbs 18:20-21 (NIV) goes on to say, *"From the fruit of their mouth a person's stomach is filled; with the harvest of their lips, they are satisfied. The tongue has the power of life and death, and those who love it will eat its fruit."*

Therefore, as kingdom citizens, it is imperative that we speak the word of God so that we are able to survive and flourish here on Earth. Our mouths (beaks) must grow and mature, meaning we cannot talk as the world talks or communicate how the world communicates. We must begin to speak the language of the Kingdom of God, which is Love, Patience, Kindness, Temperance, and Gentleness. And we communicate with others with Peace, Joy, Longsuffering, and Faithfulness.

As already mentioned, the feet of an eagle grow at a faster rate than any other part of its body. The feet are important because, according to an article written in *The Bible Vision*. The claws of an eagle are used for maintaining a firm grip while standing on rocks or other hard surfaces. They are also used for taking hold of prey during hunting activities. The claws are also used for maintaining gravity in the air while soaring. As children of God, we must have a solid grip and hold on to God's word and promises to us. God's promises must not be allowed to slip away from our eyes and our mouth. Psalms

Branching Before Flight: The Dangers of Premature Elevation

Have you been tempted to fly before you've "branched"? As wing feathers begin to grow, the eaglet waves its arms and extends them overhead in a full body stretch (which falconers call "warbling"); it then builds its breast muscles with vigorous flapping, flap-hopping, and finally catching the air to hover above the nest. From 12-16 weeks, young eagles hone flight and landing skills and experience hunting and foraging on their own for the first time. Juveniles have poor skills at this early stage, so they depend on their parents for food.(elfruler) This is why as

Christians it is very important for us to surround ourselves with other believers and get into a biblically sound church home, "The Nest," because even though we are growing and feeding ourselves spiritually (studying, praying, and fasting), our knowledge and skills are not fully developed, so we are still dependent on anointed and appointed leaders to give us proper teaching, nourishment, and correction. In other words, to be trained, equipped, and then sent out.

It is dangerous especially for newer believers to get distracted by the activities of the world or to get overly zealous about their new life in Christ and go into spheres they are not equipped or mature enough to handle, which can damage them spiritually. Eaglets, before they really fly (or fledge), have to complete a milestone activity called "branching." This is when an eaglet takes short hops/flights to branches within the nest tree. Branching usually takes 7-10 days before an eaglet takes flight. Most eaglets fledge around 12 weeks. The timing of fledging can vary from eaglet to eaglet, but it can be affected by human activity or disturbance around the nest, causing a premature fledge. This can result in the injury or even death of the eaglet. If a premature fledge (flight) happens and an eaglet falls to the ground, they can be successfully raised there for a short period by the parents, but due to no longer being at the high elevation where their nest is, predators and humans who are on the ground or lower elevations pose threats to their survival. However, an eaglet can survive and overcome this. This developmental stage of newly flighted eaglets can be a most perilous time. So, we as Christians cannot be distracted or presumptuous in our walk with Jesus, because it could cause us to fall, and the enemy is waiting for us to fall. 1

Peter 5:8-9 (NIV) warns believers to *"Be alert and of sober mind. Your enemy the devil prowls around like a roaring lion looking for someone to devour. Resist him, standing firm in the faith, because you know that the family of believers throughout the world is undergoing the same kind of sufferings."* If we as believers fall and survive being spiritually wounded or overcome the attacks of the enemy, Jesus says, *"To the one who is victorious, I will give the right to sit with me on my throne, just as I was victorious and sat down with my Father on his throne"* (Revelation 3:21 NIV). When we stay in our God-given positions (which are positions of higher elevations), we are protected from the dangers of the world seen and unseen because we are seated in heavenly places: *"And God raised us up with Christ and seated us with him in the heavenly realms in Christ Jesus"* (Ephesians 2:6 NIV).

Thermals and Trials: How Fire Lifts Us Higher

Where is God calling you to rise, not flap? We cannot get to the heights that God intends on taking us to until we learn to fly. Eagles ARE NOT chickens! When juvenile eagles turn 17-23 weeks old, they are self-sufficient and wander away from the nesting territory. But one must ask, how does an eagle gain height and altitude, unlike a chicken? The answer is that they have to elevate! So, I did some research, and what I found was so amazing and revelatory. One way that eagles can gain height/altitude is instead of using their wings and flapping they rely on rising air currents. But these aren't normal air currents. According to the American Ornithological Society, thermal updrafts allow eagles to soar higher than orographic updrafts. Thermal updrafts are rising air currents that occur when energy from the sun heats air at Earth's surface and causes it to rise. The eagle then uses this hot air to gain altitude (ELEVATE).

As the eagle uses the upward movement of the heated air to rise, sometimes God allows us to be amid the fire, and while we feel the heat as children of God, we must allow the pressure and heat of our situations/circumstances to allow our faith to rise. We must ride on the upward current of our faith and the wind of the Holy Spirit and soar above any situation/circumstance. The second revelation I received that I would like to share is remember that the above source said INSTEAD of flapping, the eagle relies on rising air currents. That statement is very powerful because it speaks to the fact that God has already given us the tools and paved the way and has already provided what we need to conquer and overcome any situation or circumstance.

Molting, Maturing, & Reproducing

What parts of your spiritual "plumage" do you feel God is shedding? As eagles grow and mature, they go through some other physiological changes. One of these changes is called molting, which is when an eagle's feathers (plumage) changes. In an article in friendsofthefoxriver.org, the writer states that a practiced eye can identify the age of a young bald eagle based on their plumage and eye and beak color. Also, plumage can indicate when they have reached the age when they can reproduce. The revelation the Lord gave me concerning this was that as we grow and mature in Him, we will have to shed some things at different stages in our kingdom journey. In each year for the first five years of its life, an eagle goes through different plumage changes. During each change, the white on the eagle's head begins to show more and more. The most dramatic change, according to friendsofthefoxriver.org, happens in the third season of an eagle's life, when it looks more calico in appearance, with its head appearing whiter. Once the eagle reaches adulthood, its color evens out, and it has the classic white head, bright-yellow beak, and beautiful brown body.

Shedding old habits for spiritual maturity will accelerate us in our Kingdom purpose; we have to get rid of the things that keep us from having a relationship with the Father. Ephesians 4:22-24 (NIV) says, *"You were taught, with regard to your former way of life, to put off your old self, which is being corrupted by its deceitful desires; to be made new in the attitude of your minds; and to put on the new self, created to be like God in true righteousness and holiness."* As we become more and more like Christ in each stage of our journey, we become brighter (as we are filled with the light of Christ). Also, our appearance becomes evident to others, as the change that is occurring on the inside is showing on the outside. As mentioned earlier, an eagle's plumage can be an indicator that it has reached the age of reproduction. As Christians, we will also reach the age of reproduction.

We are called to reproduce disciples. This is why it is important to be in alignment with mature leaders. A leader who is anointed and appointed by God will know when one of their flock is ready to reproduce because they have trained and equipped them, and the Holy Spirit has confirmed that they are ready to be sent out. *"Then Jesus came to them and said, 'All authority in heaven and on earth has been given to me. Therefore go and make disciples of all nations, baptizing them in the name of the Father and of the Son and of the Holy Spirit, and teaching them to obey everything I have commanded you. And surely I am with you always, to the very end of the age'"* (Matthew 28:18-20 NIV). As eagles reproduce and become parents, one characteristic that stood out to me was that they are very protective. As leaders, we should be protective over our less mature brothers and sisters in Christ by praying and interceding for them as they grow. The second characteristic that stood out is that they are very dedicated to their young and do all they can to endure the survival and growth of their young. As believers in Christ, we not only have to be dedicated to our own growth (reading/studying the word, worship, prayer, and fasting), but we are to our teach and encourage our brothers and sisters in Christ the importance of doing the same.

Mount Up: Your Soaring Season Is Now

I pray that this encourages you on your journey to grow and soar as an eagle. I pray that that you soar above every obstacle and circumstance that comes your way and that as you grow and mature, your Kingdom purpose will become clear. In Jesus' name, Amen.

Now is not the time to settle for the chicken coop. Now is the time to rise into the thermal currents of faith. You were made for high places. You were born to soar. Now, get ready. It is time to MOUNT UP!

ABOUT THE AUTHOR

Jasmine La Rue has been a part of the EITI since 2017. She is the founder of New Creation New Innovation Ministries and author of *I Win! The Journey of Receiving Healing and Walking in Victory*. Jasmine is a movement minister, youth leader, and community advocate. She loves the Lord, her family, and her community.

HELL IS MAD

"No More Spiritual Bullying"

Prologue

You know that feeling where you just sense that you are destined to do something great in the world, but you're not really sure what it is? That feeling when you know that you have been created differently but don't know how your differences will fit in the world, and you wonder how you will get to this version of yourself where you are operating in purpose. These are all thoughts that I had as I began my journey in the Eagles International Training Institute. Through sharing a snapshot of time on my journey, it is my hope that you will be able to take some nuggets outlined in this chapter and apply them to your own life to be able to uncover your God-given identity and stand as a divine interrupter.

The Battlefield of Life

Newly married—to my husband of five years as of the date of this writing, as we were married on February 28, 2020—I was starting afresh. I could breathe again, so I thought. My excitement was quickly met with sorrow as my childhood best friend of 30+ years passed three days later, on March 3, and two weeks later the world seemingly shut down due to COVID. This time in history was filled with fear and uncertainty. It was a time where life as "normal" for most people, including myself, was gone. As I was navigating these transitions, my grandmother took ill. Several months later, my grandmother passed on August 1 of 2020, and just when I thought that this was the worst of it, my employer at that time decided they were going to terminate me. Subsequently, on October 1 of 2020, I was given the option to leave voluntarily or get fired. This new life was not off to the start that I had imagined. The excitement that I had begun the year with was now met with grief, anger, and disappointment. So, here's the battle line: I could allow these emotions to consume me, or I could fight. But what was I fighting for, and who was I fighting?

On the surface, it appeared to be a sequence of unrelated life events; however, *appearance is not always reality*. The Word of God in the book of John 16:33 tells us that in this world we will have tribulations, distress, and suffering but to be courageous. This means we can expect that the trials and tribulations of life will come, as I have shared; however, these events can also be an entry point for the enemy to attack our mental, emotional, and spiritual life. The enemy of our soul is not just external but internal. Since our soul is comprised of our mind, will, and emotions, the enemy will use life situations to take territory in these areas. Remember when I said appearance is not reality? Well, this is because of perception; how we perceive life events is largely influenced by how we think and feel. Hence, here's a point to note: *There are things that happen* to *us and things that happen* for *us, and learning how to discern the difference will help you navigate the warfare.* This is a present-day revelation, as I did not see this when I was in the trenches of life in "my feelings." This is a slang term often used to refer to dominant negative emotions. The thing that I want you to grasp about dominant negative emotions is that they produce negative thoughts, which weaken our will to fight. This is spiritual bullying.

The enemy doesn't play fair; he never wants us to figure out how to fight. He wants to keep us in our emotions so we are fighting in the natural. The moment you learn how to war in the spirit, you become a threat to the kingdom of darkness; you become a divine interrupter. A divine interrupter is someone who disrupts and dismantles Hell's agenda, and whenever a divine interrupter is birthed in the spirit, Hell is mad!

How to Fight

There I was in grief, anger, and disappointment, but I wasn't alone. I'll say it again: I was not alone. It is important that we do not isolate ourselves from the body of Christ when we are going through difficult times. A tactic of the enemy is to get you alone in your negative thoughts and emotions, so I thank God for my husband being by my side. My kingdom marriage was divinely timed, as God had joined me with a man of great faith. Faith is not only a key to unlock your destiny; it is also a weapon against the enemy. Faith is a powerful weapon. Ephesians 6:13-17 tells us to put on the whole armor of God so that we can stand against these attacks. The shield of faith protects us and will *"extinguish all the flaming arrows of the evil one"* (AMP). I was used to fighting in the natural, but now I would learn how to use my armor to fight. God was igniting a different kind of fire in me, fueled by faith.

So, as the saying goes, I dusted myself off and reentered the workforce as a social worker at a local hospital. I started my new job at the end of October of 2020; finally a break, right? Well, that break was short-lived, but we will come back to that. I was active in my church's dance ministry during this time and had just graduated from The Eagles Network (TEN) Dance Year 2. Dancing for the Lord made me feel better; it was my place of freedom from emotional heaviness as I learned how to war with praise. Therefore, I decided to pursue additional learning of biblical dance by enrolling in the EITI's Dance Year 1 course taught by Dr. Pamela Scott. I enrolled in November of 2020. LET ME TELL YOU, I had no idea the next shift my life was getting ready to take.

I began pouring my very best into the course, studying the word of God with a fervency that I had not experienced since my days of prior collegiate graduate studies. It was as if the missing pieces of the puzzle were being put in place, and I was beginning to see the big picture. With each assignment, I flourished; my spirit was experiencing such joy. I knew then that I would be connected with Dr. Pamela in some kind of way. All that she taught resonated in my very being, and it felt like she was teaching just to me, when in reality it was a large class. I was starting to get momentum in life again, and then another obstacle … I and my entire household became sick with COVID, and my income source was in jeopardy again. The hospital's rules for COVID vaccination requirements changed from voluntary to mandated, and the job description that I was hired to do was restructured and not done so in my favor. I had fallen behind in my assignments, and catching up felt insurmountable. The pressure felt heavy. This time, however, I had more of the word of God in me; this time my faith was stronger, and Proverbs 3:5-6 became my reality. Therefore, in May of 2021, I resigned from my job to be able to focus on my spiritual growth and complete the course. Thoughts tried to come to my mind that I had made a foolish decision. However, a faith walk means you have to be okay looking crazy for Jesus, as surely this decision seemed foolish. Another point to note here is that "God moves" will always require faith, and the bigger the decision, the greater the faith needed.

Another Level in God

October of 2021, I was preparing for my final exams and week at the EITI Summit. I felt like all that I had endured, sacrificed, and overcome was culminating in this moment. Remember in the beginning when I spoke of the feeling of being destined to do great things? Well, being at Summit felt like that defining moment, where I was crossing over into another level in God. Walking across the graduation stage as Eagle Tye Mack was me soaring across the finish line. I had become an Eagle that soars!

Throughout my studies at the EITI, I was learning more about my spiritual gifts. I received a revelation about the marketplace ministry that God had called me to. It is because of this revelation that I launched my private practice, Pathway to Light Counseling Services, LLC, in December of 2021. Since its inception, God has used me to help people live a life of freedom from oppressive mental health disorders, to restore family units and marriages, and so much more!

But that was just the beginning. As the Lord would have it, my husband and I both enrolled in the School of Theology at the EITI for the upcoming school year. I did not have much time to settle in before things began to shift again. The Lord had placed it on my husband's heart to start a church in our area. He had gleaned from my journey through Dance Year 1, and the Lord revealed to him the divine connection that was to come with Dr. Pamela. As I said before, I felt I was going to be connected to her, but I didn't know how. But God sure did! The door opened with a call to serve as administrator to Dr. Pamela for the Kingdom Spheres course. I answered the call, literally! Next came the unction from my husband to meet with Dr. Pamela about being our covering to start a church.

That meeting with Dr. Pamela in February of 2022 was divinely appointed and started us on our journey to kingdom purpose as we proceeded through the Kingdom Spheres course. Another piece to the puzzle was now in place, and my, oh my, did the warfare come at my husband and I hard during this time! Our faith was stretched, and our marriage was put through the refiner's fire. The attacks came in the form of slander, financial hardship, loss of longstanding relationships, and attempts to bring disunity in our family unit, to name a few. As I stated before, when you become a divine interrupter, Hell is mad, and so was I, but with a righteous indignation. I had to discern the warfare. Was this happening *for* me or *to* me? Was this from God or the enemy? Here's a point to note: If it's happening *for* you, then there is something that

God has for you to get out of the situation to better you in some way. If it's happening *to* you, then you have to remember that the attitude of your mind and heart can win or lose the battle. This doesn't mean that we won't feel the pressure; nor will we enjoy it, but we will win when we learn how to discern in the spirit and not stay stuck in our feelings. I'll say it again: *appearance is not always reality*; how we perceive the warfare is key. The battle to win is the one over your mind, will, and emotions, not your money, relationships, or reputation.

So, we locked into the word of God and remained steadfast in our faith, fervent in prayer, and committed to the vision He had given us. Romans 5:3-4 (NLT) says to *"rejoice, too, when we run into problems and trials, for we know that they help us develop endurance. And endurance develops strength of character..."*; we surely had many character-building moments. The Kingdom Spheres course was shifting my mindset of church as usual to apostolic wineskin. The course was equipping and maturing me spiritually, and I was receiving more and more revelation on God's kingdom and my place in. It is by God's revelation to us that we received the heavenly blueprint to launch our ministry, Access Granted Ministries, Inc., an apostolic center, in 2022. Once again, I soared across the finish line but this time together with my husband.

Still Soaring

My journey is far from over, and the warfare is still strong, but I am beyond grateful to have Dr. Pamela as my spiritual mother. Dr. Pamela was instrumental in helping me navigate through the storm. She was the voice of peace when I needed it and the hand of guidance when I was unsure. She also gave me the push out of the nest when I was afraid to leave the familiar place. It is from her teachings and impartation that I not only learned the difference between having a covering and being in alignment but experienced it.

I have often heard Dr. Pamela say, and I paraphrase, as kingdom ambassadors, we don't just take what comes our way, but we have the power to create what comes. This means that we are not to succumb to spiritual bullying.

Earlier in the chapter, I posed the questions, "What am I fighting for, and who am I fighting?" I would like to answer those now. First, we are fighting to reclaim territory, not just geographical but spiritual, emotional, and mental. Second, *"We are not fighting against flesh-and-blood enemies, but against evil rulers and authorities of the unseen world ..."* (Ephesians 6:12 NLT). Emotions such as fear, doubt, discouragement, anxiety, and anger are some of the most common warfare you will experience. This warfare is designed to keep the real you oppressed to limit your spiritual growth, but it is time to shift and grow!

Soar Beyond

Here's what I want to leave you with. The way to soar beyond is to see each situation as an opportunity to uncover the God in you. Your Godly character is your true identity! God has created His children to be divine interrupters! When we truly understand that the weapons of our warfare are not carnal but mighty through God to the pulling down of strongholds, and that we should be casting down imaginations ... and bringing into captivity every thought to the obedience to Christ (2 Corinthians 10:4-5), we are now operating in spiritual discernment instead of carnal warfare.

If you are reading this book, it means NOW is the time for you to operate in another level of freedom. It's time for you to soar higher and come up out of the trenches of life. Don't allow life situations, challenges, or negative emotions to hold you down. Soar above your current state. Read Isaiah 40:31, be willing to shift, be okay looking crazy for Jesus, and most importantly, stay armed in the Word.

It's time for you to disrupt Hell's agenda! NO more spiritual bullying!

ABOUT THE AUTHOR

Tye Mack, native of Flint, MI, is a devoted wife, mother, and servant leader. Tye received her ordination and licensing from the Eagles International Training Institute as a Licensed Minister of Dance in 2021 and was ordained Apostle in 2022. She is also an entrepreneur who established Pathway to Light Counseling Services, LLC.

IN THE BEGINNING

I was a rambunctious youth back in the early 70s, and my church pastor's wife, Mary Jacobs, owned one of the first studios in Atlanta to train girls of color in the city. During a Sunday service, she told my grandmother that she needed to enroll me in dance, since I had "so much energy and could not keep still in church." Needless to say, this pivotal moment at the age of six would be life-changing: the catalyst that launched me to "dancing in church."

I studied dance for many years through elementary school up to high school. Although I lost my mother in sixth grade, I was inspired to continue to pursue my love of dance by my high school dance teacher, Muriel Odum. I was one of four minority students from the public school system to be chosen for the illustrious Governor's Honors program in Dance in the tenth grade. By my senior year, my journey would take a different path, as I became a teenage mother during that year. However, Ms. Odum was by my side every step of the way and never let me stop dancing.

I went on to graduate with honors (top 10% of the class), danced at my high school graduation, and begin college that fall. I opted to attend a small liberal arts college that did not offer dance so that I could stay focused and finish my college education. I was determined to silence all of the naysayers and the "old church ladies" who labeled me as "fast" and who thought that my choices had derailed my future. But God. The experience and comments from members of the church that I had grown up in were hurtful and in some cases outright mean. They ultimately caused me to withdraw from attending church regularly as I had with my grandmother for so many years, and I was away from the church for 10-plus years.

I finished my undergraduate and graduate degree before I actually reconnected with a church that ultimately became the place and space where I felt safe and accepted regardless of my past. My exposure to dance ministry was birthed there. My journey with Eagles International Training Institute began in 2004, when I attended an Eagles Advance with Apostle Pamela Scott. Dr. Pamela (as she was known at that time) was one of the first "generals" of dance ministry I was introduced to shortly after joining the dance ministry. The ministry leader shared with me that while I was beautifully, technically trained, I needed greater understanding of the purpose of my movements and how I could use my training to preach the gospel. Hold up ... preach? Who, me? No way! I sinned and I am not qualified to preach ...! Or so I thought.

While I faithfully danced before the congregation on a regular basis, I had absolutely no desire to speak in front of them. I frequently taught movement, leadership, and biblical foundations for dancers all across the United States, but I still had a fear of speaking before my church body. Then, it finally happened. I received a call from our ministry Elder requesting that I preach. I must have cried for three days straight. Even though I thought of every reason why the elder should pick someone else, I wrote out my message, had five different people critique it, and still felt inadequate to go before God's people and deliver a sermon.

The morning of the sermon message, I cried for 40 minutes before I went into the sanctuary. I felt troubled that I was not prepared enough and would embarrass myself. For many years, Proverbs 3:5-6 (NIV) had been my "go to" scripture: *"Trust in the LORD with all your heart and lean not on your own understanding; in all your ways submit to him, and he will make your paths straight"*. But I failed to realize that Proverbs 3:5-6 was manifesting itself through me at that very moment. My "aha" moment came when I realized that everything, and I do mean everything, in my life had prepared me for that moment. The sermon's title was "When you can't see your ditches," and the sermon theme focused on when things are before you that you can't really see, God already has a plan to detour you around them. While the detour may take you on a longer route, you can reach your destination; you just see it from a different perspective.

The Journey

Our experiences might not be completely comprehensible most of the time, but there is a purpose for each encounter and a lesson to be learned from them all. After Jesus was baptized, the next thing He experienced was temptation. Even Jesus Christ is led into the wilderness by the Holy Spirit, where he is tempted by

Satan, His adversary. Likewise, the nature of our own wilderness experiences means that we often question why we were brought to certain places, down certain paths, or directly stand in the face of adversity. Why me, Lord?

As with the Jews, the wilderness can evoke many emotions and memories. Most familiar is their 40-year journey out of Egypt. What we must come to accept is that the wilderness is a place of vulnerability, a difficult experience in an unfamiliar place with uncertain provisions (Exodus 15:22-24; 16:2-3). In that story, the wilderness was a place of testing where the promises of God were all they had (Deuteronomy 8:1-5). The wilderness was not just a place of vulnerability for the Jews. It was also a place of transition that lay between their slavery and liberation (Exodus 3:17). Jesus' wilderness experience marked a transition for Him too. Sometimes we must recognize that the wilderness experience is a point of preparation for the place where we are being elevated and exposed.

The wilderness can be a dark, frightful, lonely place that causes you anxiety and fear because of the multitude of unknown dangers. We must continue to recognize who God was to Israel and who He is to us individually. As you remember Jesus Christ, our deliverer, you might realize that your wilderness experience may actually prove to be your transition into an unprecedented period of fruitfulness. I too found myself in this wilderness.

How do we get oppressed in our mindset, thoughts, and actions? While there are a number of definitions of the word "oppressed," the one that struck a chord with me was "the state of being subject to unjust treatment or control." Oppression is synonymous with persecution, abuse, maltreatment, suppression, subjection, cruelty, brutality, injustice, hardship, suffering, misery, mental pressure, and distress.

When I think about the number of disloyal friendships, bad and unhealthy relationships, missed promotional opportunities at work, and loss of loved ones, I have experienced as well as the countless times my efforts and achievements have been overlooked or gone unrecognized by someone, or someone else has taken credit for the work that I did, it seemed easy for me to get to a place of oppression and have a difficult time moving on. I even took the position, "Why should I do any more? It's not worth it." But God showed me differently. I am worth it to Him and to the Kingdom.

This period of transition and transformation was pivotal in teaching me and revealing to me that God is faithful when we genuinely and authentically serve Him. God does not let disappointment and hurt keep us down for too long. Through my journey in the wilderness, I had to recognize His hand in every situation and understand His protection. Some of the dysfunction and the disruptive and disturbing experiences I encountered were really the canvas for building my character. I learned a lot from those experiences, and so will you.

The Calling

The prophet Jeremiah is known as a faithful servant who courageously and faithfully declared God's word despite at times being alone in declaring his message. Jeremiah's early messages were a call to repentance for condemnation of Judah for their false worship and social injustices. Jeremiah's prophecies had been critical of the people's dependence on the temple as a place of security and their selfishness and materialism, much like many of us who rely on the security of tangible things as a source of our comfort and protection. Jeremiah often preached messages of doom, and the messages were full of bad news. Jeremiah was not a popular messenger, but he was prophetic. Jeremiah had his prophetic writings burned, was thrown into prison, and then was later tossed into a cistern. Jeremiah also suffered from internal doubt and conflict about what he had been called to do.

Now how many of us have days like Jeremiah's, when everything someone says or does is negative? How many times have we questioned ourselves when God directed us to do something, or even questioned that it was really God? The thing we can learn from Jeremiah's character is that Jeremiah believed in his messages, and he had a determined resolve and passion to compel people to change their ways.

When he started on his journey, Jeremiah probably did not expect to encounter the roadblocks, distractions, obstacles, and challenges he did, but he remained obedient to his call. God ultimately rewarded Jeremiah because of his obedience, despite what others had to say. Jeremiah realized that his assignment was bigger than who he was and how other people perceived him, and Jeremiah fully operated in his prophetic calling. He was special and knew his gift was special; therefore, he aspired to being more than just average or mediocre.

Many times we are faced with difficult situations in life. We feel lonely, as if we are the only ones experiencing this challenge. We ask the question, "Why did this happen to me?" The path we are on may seem dark, dismal, and as if there is no way out. But ditches and potholes show up unexpectedly, and when they do, they grab our attention. There are times when God is intentionally trying to grab our attention to enable us to take some action.

There was a plan. God was protecting me all the time. I just needed to declare to myself that God's word said that His plan was to prosper me and not to harm me. I also had to remind myself in this situation to *"Trust in the Lord with all thine heart; and lean not unto thine own understanding. In all thy ways acknowledge him and he shall direct your paths,"* as is written in Proverbs 3:5-6 (KJV). When I began to realize God's real plan for me, I had to know that it was Him that I needed to trust to deal with that situation.

Once you begin to know that you know, you will begin to realize that in the midst of your worse situations—loss of a job, loss of a loved one, depression, sickness, financial difficulties, loneliness—you should not forget that God does have a plan. The situations and circumstances that come up in our lives are indeed a setup. Sometimes God needs to get our attention quickly. Sometimes He will let things happen in a subtle way, and sometimes it is not so subtle.

The Exodus/Into the Promised Land

Life experiences and scriptures have revealed to us that after a period of joy and blessing, we will eventually enter a dry wilderness. This is not to say that we will be dry spiritually. Depending upon how we allow life to happen and how we manage what happens, we could be dry mentally, physically, emotionally, and spiritually.

God's will for us is to be filled with the Holy Spirit (Ephesians 5:18), and He does not withhold the Holy Spirit from those who obey Him. The Holy Spirit is the one who encourages us in good times and bad times. Let me be clear, even with the Holy Spirit, it is possible to go through a wilderness experience in which there is almost nothing in your circumstances to encourage you. There are times when you may just try to survive from day to day, emotionally, financially, or materially. You are waiting for your healing to manifest. Your joy and peace have been violated by unfavorable emotions and thoughts, which you must gather the strength to resist. It is difficult, but remember God's promise that you will never be tempted beyond your ability to endure, and with each temptation, He will also make a way of escape, that you may be able to bear it.

During this season of testing and trials, you will find the ordinary comforts of the world will not satisfy you. This is the time when you are forced to depend on God for all you need emotionally, physically, and spiritually. Proverbs 3:5-6 reminds us to trust that the wilderness time is only temporary and to diligently trust God for direction.

As I matriculated through the various opportunities for training through the EITI, I began to discover my voice and my purpose. Starting in Dance Year 1 helped me to identify how to use my God-given talent along with my many years of technical training and to not to feel insecure about my training. I learned how to dance the story and to deliver the message more fully through movement. The EITI also helped me find my voice of intercession and prayer and learn how to intimately commune with the Father so that my movement through dance and movement through life became more authentic and genuine as my spiritual relationship grew.

This journey out of the wilderness and into God's promises is directly connected to my exposure and experience through the EITI. What started as a pursuit of increasing and building my knowledge and skills as a dancer evolved into finding and developing my spiritual knowledge and developing more confidence. The experience helped me soar into my teaching, prophetic, and preaching gifts and become a better servant leader by sitting at the feet of wise teachers who graciously imparted, shared, pushed, and pulled me spiritually and personally to grow and challenge myself in preparation for God's mission in my life. Your wilderness experience too is purposefully designed to help you gain a deeper reliance on God and His character so that you develop into and demonstrate those characteristics in your walk.

Wilderness experiences often involve challenges and tests that build character and strength. God can use wilderness experiences to prepare individuals for their future roles and responsibilities. The wilderness can be a time of waiting, and it can teach individuals to trust God's timing and to not rush ahead but rather to rely on Him. Walk into His Promises and Soar!

ABOUT THE AUTHOR

Tonya R. McClure is a native of Atlanta, GA, a mother of one son, Ricky, "T-Ma" to Reese and Ryan, and MIL to Tiffany. Tonya is an ordained Elder, competitive dance coach, published author, Alpha Eagle '06, and Human Resources professional. She loves to travel, walk 5ks, and plan events.

THE UNFOLDING MAJESTY

Each feather that forms, each lesson carried by the wind, speaks of the eagle's unfolding majesty. It was never meant to crawl or perch; it was Destined to Soar. I too learned that I was destined to soar.

My journey mirrors that of an eagle. In the early seasons, I mistook comfort for safety. I stayed in places for longer than I should have, afraid to step out, believing the ground was all I deserved. Pride, fear, insecurity: They each wove threads into my life, but not without leaving their marks.

Born-to-soar hatchling/newly hatched eaglets are covered in downy feathers and are dependent on their parents for everything. Growing up in Florida's Historic District of Goldsboro, I was always on the go: running, dancing, joking, and laughing at everything or nothing at all. Curious and carefree, I was joy in motion. If fun could be found, I'd find it. If a reaction could be sparked, I was going for it. Even then, I carried a spark.

But my world wasn't just play. I was raised in a Christian home—a household anchored in faith. Church wasn't optional;

it was a way of life. Sunday morning services, choir rehearsals, late-night revivals, and bible study were woven into my routine like favorite spirituals on repeat.

Like the eagle that builds its nest, safe, secure, and surrounded by sky, my mother and grandparents' home was my spiritual high place. A refuge where my faith took root.

"As an eagle stirreth up her nest, fluttereth over her young, spreadeth abroad her wings, taketh them, beareth them on her wings" (Deuteronomy 32:11 KJV).

The Lord was preparing me: nestled in love, destined to soar. Like an eagle raised high in the cleft of the rock, my spirit was being formed in elevation.

Transitional Stage

As eaglets grow, they develop more feathers, and their downy feathers are replaced with juvenile feathers. When I was eight years old, my mother felt inspired to move in hopes of finding better opportunities for herself and for me. We relocated to Springfield, Massachusetts. It was a complete culture shock! As a little girl who grew up in Florida, I spoke with a southern drawl and often felt awkward in northern settings. I was self-conscious about my shape and thick, kinky curls, but I kept it hidden. On the outside, I appeared confident, ambitious, and always moving toward something greater.

I found myself surrounded by a different culture of people, and a different way of life, including a different dialect of language.

Whenever the children around me heard me speak, they would pause. Something was different. It was my southern drawl—a sound that, for me, brought a sense of uneasiness. I remember listening closely and learning quickly how to speak with a northern dialect. I felt like all eyes were on me, even though, in reality, they weren't. But I was able to conquer the fear of sounding and feeling awkward.

As eagles grow, they flap and stretch their wings in the nest, preparing for flight. That's how I see my own growth. One of my most memorable stretching moments came after attending a Frank Hatchett dance recital. My mom asked if I wanted to dance; I said yes. I was excited inside but nervous outside. That first class was nerve-racking and uncertain. But just like an eagle can't fly by staying in the nest, God began to stir me, removing comfort to build strength. He was preparing me for the journey of my life.

My first year in dance class felt awkward. I was the biggest student in the room. Despite how I felt, I was placed front and center so others could follow me. I often watched the Junior Dance Team, dreaming of one day dancing with them. It was my fledgling season. In my second year, I entered a phase of real development. I was selected for the Semi-Junior Team. Even then, as a child, I realized God was the wind beneath my wings.

Life's journey continued as my mother and I returned to Florida. I came back more confident and courageous. As a pre-teen, teen, and young adult, I felt unstoppable; and I tried to be. I jumped into everything: cheerleading, basketball, softball, band; and I would have played football if they allowed girls. During this stage, I stumbled, fell, and made plenty of mistakes, but it was all part of my growth (Psalm 34:19).

The Season of Wandering/ Straying from the Covering

As a young adult, I was running and chasing self, flesh, and whatever felt good in the moment. Though I was raised under the safety of faith, I stepped outside of that covering. My mother's prayers, my grandparent's wisdom, church teachings, and the word were still there, but I wasn't surrendered. I knew of God, but I wasn't committed to His leading. Like an eagle that leaves the heights too soon, I became vulnerable. Young eagles don't soar until they learn to ride the wind. I was trying to fly on my own, outside the wind of the Holy Spirit (Proverbs 14:12).

The Major Awakening

Then came a moment that shook me to the core. Everything I had been running from, hiding behind, and avoiding came crashing down at once. I felt completely out of order. Emotionally and mentally, I was in a place I never imagined. I was with child. I didn't think I would survive the birth. Not because of the pregnancy, but because of the emotional weight I carried. Shame, fear, and regret buried me. *"The sorrows of death encompassed me"* (Psalm 116:3 KJ21); the guilt was suffocating. It felt like God allowed everything to stop just to get my attention.

Like a wounded eagle returning to the nest, I had to face the brokenness in me. Deep down, I longed for change. With an eager plea and an open heart, I surrendered to Jesus Christ. He brought me up out of a horrible pit, out of the miry clay; He set my feet upon a rock and established my goings.

What should have been the end became the beginning of my walk with God. In that valley, I realized His grace still reached me. He never stopped loving me, and He never will. Just as the eagle uses the storm to rise, God used my brokenness to draw me in, align me, reshape me, and prepare me to soar.

In my journey, I knew the Lord was with me. Wherever you are at the moment, give it to Jesus. Allow the Holy Spirit to pour for the soar.

From Brokenness to Blessing: A Celebration of Praise

One of the greatest blessings was born out of a dark and uncertain time. What the enemy meant for shame and sorrow, God turned into a testimony of Salvation and New Birth. This was a divine interruption, a season of praise. The Unfolded Majesty. God is our Redeemer. He doesn't throw us away when we fall. He gently restores us, making all things new.

> *"To appoint unto them that mourn in Zion to give unto them beauty for ashes, the oil of joy for mourning, the garment of praise for the spirit of heaviness"* (Isaiah 61:3 KJV).

Like the eagle emerging from the storm, I came out stronger, clearer, on to rise.

"But those who trust in the Lord will find new strength. They will soar high on wings like eagles. They will run and not grow weary. They will walk and not faint" (Isaiah 40:31 NLT).

A New Season: Moving in Grace and Growing in Worship
Standing Strong and Set Apart

Even after the joy of discovering my place in ministry, life didn't stop bringing challenges. One of the hardest storms I had to endure was the failure of my marriage. I didn't see it coming. I prayed. I hoped. But in the end, it unraveled. And though my heart broke, God's mercy remained. The enemy tried to use that season to conquer me, to silence my praise and shut down my purpose. But he failed. Through every tear, lonely night, and moment of questioning, God upheld me. I continued to minister, dance, and believe. Even when shame whispered lies, I silenced them with praise.

> *"But he said to me, 'My grace is sufficient for you, for my power is made perfect in weakness.' Therefore I will boast all the more gladly about my weaknesses, so that Christ's power may rest on me"* (2 Corinthians 12:9 NIV).

Years passed; the pain didn't disappear overnight, but God gave me strength, wisdom, and knowledge. He graced me to nurture my children, not in fear or bitterness, but in love and reverence for Him. I poured into them what had been poured into me.

And now, I see them growing as God-fearing, loving individuals shaped by prayer and anchored in truth.

> *"For your Maker is your husband—the Lord Almighty is his name—the Holy One of Israel is your Redeemer"* (Isaiah 54:5 NIV).

Tribe of Judah Dance Ministry

Ministering in dance at Word of Faith Family Worship Cathedral Austell, GA, for over 20 years, this is where my foundation in praise and worship dance was formed. In the beginning, I was drawn to the freedom I saw in others, my love of the art of dance, and how their movement flowed with the Spirit, expressing what words often could not.

Another deep struggle came in answering my call to the ministry of dance. I knew God had breathed life into it. It was in my bones, worship, and tears, but it was not always received by those around me. I carried an ache of being misunderstood, overlooked, and sometimes even dismissed. It was a lonely road at times, dancing in the presence of One, trusting that even if man did not affirm it, God had already appointed and anointed it. Even rejection became another gust of wind, another invitation to rise higher, to dance not for applause but in His glory alone.

With years of experience, I longed for a deeper understanding of what it truly meant to minister in dance; this led me to EITI.

EITI: Eagles International Training Institute: Clarity of the Lift

This was more than a program. It was a divine appointment. A spiritual boot camp.

My first class, I knew I was in the right place. The training was intense, not just physically or intellectually but also spiritually. Every lesson, assignment, moment spent in prayer and study stirred something deep inside me. There was a divine eagerness ignited in me, a fire to fulfill the call God placed on my life. I learned prophetic dance expressing movement that communicated a message of truth to others. As I served faithfully, God began to reveal the ministry intercession in motion, breakthrough through movement, and healing through praise. I found joy in surrendering myself as a vessel, allowing the Holy Spirit to guide every move.

The more I gave myself to the call, the more the anointing grew. Through EITI, my direction became clearer. I wasn't just dancing; I was truly ministering in dance; I was soaring with intentionality. Like an eagle in training, I learned how to stretch my wings, how to fly at higher altitudes without fear. I learned the discipline it takes to be effective in ministry and the humility it takes to carry the anointing. *"The Lord directs the steps of the godly. He delights in every detail of their lives"* (Psalm 37:23 NLT). I thank You, Father, for Your divine direction. For not leaving me wandering or guessing. For leading me, training me, and equipping me through the institute that carries the very name of what I'm called to be: an EAGLE.

SOARING WITH PURPOSE

There were times I almost gave up, times when the battle in my mind told me that I would never soar, that my mistakes had clipped my wings forever. I fought with doubt, with comparison, and with feelings of unworthiness.

I often reflect on the eagle. Not just because the Bible uses it as a symbol of strength and renewal, but because I see myself in the journey. Eagles are not like other birds. When storms come, most birds seek shelter, but not the eagle. The eagle flies directly into the storm, using the strong winds to lift itself higher. It spreads its wings and lets the force of the wind carry it above the clouds. What others run from, the eagle rises through. That is the testimony.

There are seasons of life when the winds of life beat hard against you: broken relationships, emotional exhaustion, career frustrations, and personal battles. But instead of crashing, learn to spread your wings. Learn to trust God to carry you (Psalm 18:33).

Like the eaglet, I didn't always feel ready to soar. But the storm pushed me into a place where I had no choice but to rise. To trust the air of the Holy Spirit beneath me. To let go of fear, shame, and doubt, and fly.

> *"They that wait upon the Lord shall renew their strength; they shall mount up with wings as eagles; they shall run, and not be weary; and they shall walk, and not faint"* (Isaiah 40:31 KJV).

The tapestry of my life is not neat or pristine. It is stained with tears, mended with grace, and strengthened through storms.

Every thread, even the ones born from my mistakes, has been redeemed by the Master Weaver's hand. He has taught me that failure is not fatal when it is placed at His feet. He has shown me that brokenness can still birth beauty.

Every storm I faced was never meant to break me; it was designed to teach me how to soar higher. It was in the turbulence that my wings grew strong and my vision sharpened; in letting go, my spirit learned to rise.

Today, I stand not because I've mastered flight but because I've surrendered to the wind of His Spirit. My story is still unfolding. My majesty is still being revealed. And just like the eagle, I know I was never created to settle. I was never made to crawl. *I was Destined to Soar.*

AND SO ARE YOU!

My life is a testament to what happens when you don't give up. You were not created to remain grounded by fear, failure, or the opinions of others. The same hands that wove strength into my wings are weaving it into yours. Every tear, trial, and triumph are preparing you for the heights you were born to reach.

There is majesty unfolding inside of you even now. Don't despise the winds; let them lift you. Don't fear the storms; they are building your strength. You have been called higher and crafted for more.

Let God lift, guide, and direct your flight. Spread your wings! *YOU ARE DESTINED TO SOAR!*

ABOUT THE AUTHOR

Revonda A. McKnight, M.Ed., Educator, EITI Eagle Graduate, Fashion Designer, Minister of Dance, and Founder of Divine Dance Designs by Von. She passionately ministers healing through education, dance, and recreation, using inspiration as a divine tool for empowerment, restoration, and spiritual transformation: a gift inspired through her faith-driven approach to life, the arts, and education.

YOUR RISE TO SOAR IS NO ACCIDENT: IT'S INTENTIONAL, DESIRABLE, AND FORTUNATE!

"Behold, I am making all things new"

(Revelation 21:5 ESV)

There I was, upside down, disoriented, and wondering what just happened. "God, am I still alive?" From where I was situated, after the car landed on its roof, I could see feet walking around the car and hear voices in a panic: "Hurry, we need to get her out of there!" "Is she alive?"

The voice of God answered … "She is alive!" The disorientation settled enough for me to realize I had been in a terrible accident.

Nearly tragic, not only did this accident leave me with a broken C2 vertebra in three places, but it also left me with a broken spirit and a ton of questions, with the major one being, "God, why did this happen to me?" In an instant, physical pain with a broken neck and emotional pain with a deep sense of loss, despair, and feelings of hopelessness had become my portion. It would take countless days and nights before things seemed normal again. Notice I said, "seemed normal." Although I was alive, I felt like I had died, and at that time, I did not understand how this feeling was significant and that it would be the first experience of losing the old me.

The old me was satisfied with where I was in life. Having grown up in a dysfunctional family where alcoholism and drugs ruled, I had defied the odds of becoming a product of my environment. I acknowledged that it was God who removed me from that toxic situation, and I believed that I was better off than those I left behind. *I survived!* I had every reason to feel content with where I was, and for a time that was enough! But God refused to let me stay there. God revealed to me that He is my creator, and He did not want me to live life aimlessly, believing that where I was at that time in my life was my final destination. He wanted me to understand that the rest of the life he had designed for me was just beginning, but in order to receive this new life, the old me had to die.

What's Your Story?

It is no accident that you are reading my chapter in this anthology. I believe that you have been divinely led here because you have your own story. Have you been dealt an unfair hand in life? Maybe you have experienced the loss of a job, or you have been given an unexpected medical diagnosis or even had an accident similar to mine. Whatever your story, I hope that you will find solace and understanding in these few pages and gain a renewed hope to know that *"The Lord is close to the brokenhearted and saves those who are crushed in spirit"* (Psalm 34:18 NIV). It will get better, and there is a new YOU arising!

DEFINING THE ACCIDENT (IT'S INTENTIONAL!)

Dictionary.com defines an "accident" as an "undesirable or unfortunate happening that occurs unintentionally and usually results in harm, injury, damage, or loss; casualty; mishap." Accidents and incidents in life are bound to happen. Unfortunately, there is no way around them. Jesus spoke to his disciples saying, *"I have told you these things so that in me you might have peace. In this world you will have trouble. But take heart! I have overcome the world"* (John 16:33 NIV). Jesus Christ gave his life for our sin and salvation; therefore, there is nothing He is not able to redeem us from. As Christians, we are reminded that the trials and tribulations we face in this life are opportunities for us to gain greater strength to soar (James 1: 2-4).

It is quite natural for us to see accidents and incidents in our lives at their face value. They interrupt life and shatter dreams, making it difficult, especially when we are in the midst of them, to see them as anything else. This is where our faith in God has to take over. God has no intention to harm us but every intention to prosper us (Jeremiah 29:11). He does not always allow situations to occur, but His divine orchestration leads us to a greater purpose. God showed me clearly that the accident that happened to me was NO ACCIDENT! It was a turning point in my life and an intentional part of His plan to start me on a journey with Him that would interrupt my complacency and move me in the direction of the greater calling in my life. So you see, it matters how we define our accidents and incidents in life. According to God's Word, it will all work out in the end (Romans 8:28).

The "MORE-PH" – God's Grace and Help to Heal

> *This is what I call the "MORE-ph"—a season when God is not only healing you but also morphing you into more than you were. More grace. More strength. More purpose.*

I wish that I could tell you that things got better for me. Miraculously, I was spared from becoming a quadriplegic, and my broken C2 vertebra healed without surgery. That's good news! But my self-esteem and my spirit were still shattered and I did not know that it would be a long journey before I found my new self. During my healing process, and even for some time after, several other losses surfaced that kept me drawing closer to the Lord. My mother passed away, my family lost their home, and as a result, I lost my stability, my sense of belonging and security, and I gained a whole lot of uncertainty. This loss included losing continuity in my family relationships. Then, to make things worse, when I needed friends to stick closer to me than a brother, I lost a whole entire circle of people whom I thought were my friends. I found out quickly that Jesus was the only one I could totally rely upon (Proverbs 18:24).

I remember the actual moment I felt God's strength underneath me. It made me press into Him and desire Him all the more. I realized that I was at the lowest point in my life! I was broken, and I was young. I felt abandoned, especially since my father and my mother were no longer living. It was then that I knew that if this friend named Jesus was sticking close to me, I in turn had better stick closer to Him. The Lord was my only hope. So in my desperation, I sought Him for answers, advice, and direction. I needed God and His sufficient grace to hold me and to heal me. "Just to be close to you is my desire"—I found myself singing that song by CeCe Winans and praying that prayer every day!

I fully yielded and fully surrendered myself to Him. I gave Him the accident, the incidents, the problems, the hurts, the fears, the brokenness, the uncertainty, and the sorrows, and then I began to notice something wonderful happening … *I started to soar* (Isaiah 40:31)! It seemed so instant. The weights were removed, and I felt myself being able to move and breathe again (Acts 17:28)! He gave me a sense of clarity! I could hear Him, and I could feel Him helping me! I could feel Him changing me! The healing had begun and it was time to figure out my next!

Your rise to soar is no accident. God is near, and He is waiting for your surrender. What will you give completely to Him so that you can experience His grace to heal?

Pray with me:

> *Father, help me to see beyond what I see in the natural world as accidents. Teach me to trust that You are at work even in the chaos, the pain, and the unforeseen trials of life. I surrender anything that is not acceptable in me to*

You so I can heal. I give You the old me so You can make me new. Amen!

TIME TO SOAR! (IT'S DESIRABLE!)

I had never paid much attention to eagles before and certainly never saw myself as one. To me, an eagle was just another bird among many that God had created. But as I have come to see, even that changed perspective was part of His divine plan.

It was no accident that I ended up at a dance conference in Mansfield, Ohio, the very place where I met Apostle Dr. Pamela Scott and, at the time, just a few individuals known as "eagles." "Eagle" was the name given to those who understood they were created to carry great vision and to reflect God's strength, resilience, and power on Earth. That moment, over 20 years ago, was divinely orchestrated. Today, I stand in awe along with many others at how that single encounter has flourished into a global family of bold, beautiful eagle people soaring around the world. I am deeply grateful to God and feel truly blessed to have met her during one of the lowest seasons of my life.

God used her to speak purpose and destiny into me. With her love and passion for mentoring, she nurtured my spiritual growth and helped me deepen my relationship with the Lord, guiding me to use my spiritual gifts for a greater Kingdom purpose here on Earth. My journey with the Eagles International Training Institute and what we lovingly call our Eagle family is where I discovered that I was born to soar. It was there that I finally embraced the call to walk in my God-given purpose.

So I accepted this opportunity from God to become Eagle Sentheia! Desiring to know more, I set out to learn about this powerful, majestic bird, the eagle, which represents vision, strength, resilience, and confidence. I had a desire to learn, and it was just what I needed. One of the most important things I learned is that the eagle understands how to use thermal currents to spread its wings and soar high above perilous storms. It goes through a molting process, which is very much like a transformation or a spiritual journey of dying to self. During this time, the eagle loses its feathers and its beak and becomes isolated and vulnerable. It is almost like it is coming to the end of its life. Eventually, after this time of great weakness, it begins to experience a regrowth of new feathers, a new beak, and a new ability to fly to greater heights. It emerges even stronger and more beautiful than before. This process resonated deeply with me. God was clearly giving me vision to see the beautiful *new me* that was starting to emerge!

IT'S FOR YOU TOO!

I believe every life has purpose, and while we live our lives on Earth, God wants us to use our gifts to serve Him and others. I often reflect on the stories of Job and Joseph in the Bible. While their stories are very different, they both were able to soar above their circumstances because of the way they responded to their trials. How are you responding to your trials? Job and Joseph acknowledged their losses and surrendered to their own "molting process," all in exchange for a transformative and closer walk with God, a greater sense of clarity in their callings, and a renewed strength for the journey. For them, loss was not their end but the beginning of a greater purpose that God had prepared. Just as these stories have given me hope, I pray they inspire you too. Loss, accidents, incidents, and life's battles are never your final chapter because YOU were born to soar. *"And after you have suffered a little while, the God of all grace, who has called you to his eternal glory in Christ, will restore, confirm, strengthen, and establish you."* (1 Peter 5:10 ESV).

New Life, New Dance! (IT'S FORTUNATE!)

You have power over the enemy! When you truly recognize this, your words and actions change, and the devil's plans unravel! The devil had a chance to destroy me, and he nearly did, but God's plan for my life was far greater, and it included me living well beyond December 10, 1999. The same is true for you! YOU ARE ALIVE! Now that you have realized this truth, speak boldly to the enemy and remind him of God's Word. *"You intended to harm me, but God intended it for good to accomplish what is now being done, the saving of many lives"* (Genesis 50:20 NIV).

This scripture and many others have become powerful weapons in my arsenal. It is the Word of God that gives me strength and keeps me in flight. With the help and guidance of the Holy Spirit, my wisdom, knowledge, understanding, and discernment continue to grow in precision, and I can spot the enemy's attacks dead on!

This is my new life, and with it, I have a new dance. Not just movement on a stage, but a rhythm of living that flows with purpose, praise, and power. Every step I take now is intentional. Every breath is a celebration. I dance because *I survived*. The voice of God answered ... "She is alive." *I AM alive!* My life is the choreography of God's grace and a testimony of God's mercy.

As I reflect on the goodness of God, I am overwhelmed by all that awaited me—and what has now become my portion because I chose to live life on purpose. No longer homeless, I purchased my own home. I pursued my education and earned three degrees. I completed seminary and I am now a licensed minister, pastor, and leader in ministry. God's blessings have opened doors for me to share His love and to preach, teach, and dance in other nations and to connect with a family far beyond my biological one.

I am positively shaping the minds and futures of the next generation, fulfilling the purpose God has set before me. This isn't about boasting; it's about joy and gratitude. I give all honor and glory to God for sending me as His ambassador to help advance His plan of salvation in the world.

I love the new me. I am *SENTheia!* Called and sent. I am not only fortunate to know the Lord but also favored to know that MY RISE TO SOAR IS NO ACCIDENT. And neither is yours!

> *"These trials are only to test your faith, to see whether or not it is strong or pure. It is being tested as fire tests gold and purifies it----and your faith is far more precious to God than mere gold; so if your faith remains strong after being tried in the test tube of fiery trials, it will bring you much praise and glory and honor on the day of his return." (1 Peter 1:7-9 Living Bible)*

ABOUT THE AUTHOR

 Sentheia McLeod, AKA "Pastor SENT," is a pastor, dance leader, author, educator, and mentor. She serves in leadership at the Eagles International Training Institute. Her passion to motivate and inspire young lives has led her to teach and author her first book titled, *New Life, New Dance*. She enjoys traveling and sharing the gospel of Jesus wherever she goes!

DIVINE DATE OF DESTINY

THE FALLING OF THE APOSTOLIC MANTLE
Eiti Torah And Anointing Instructor
Becoming An Eagle In October Of 2009

It was in the summer of 2005 that I met Apostle Dr. Pamela Scott at a dance conference in Dallas, Texas. This conference was hosted by the National Liturgical Dance Network (NLDN) Conference and was my first exposure of its kind.

In 2001, I was installed as the dance director for the Cornerstone Church Rejoice Dance Team. The team only ministered during the Feast of Tabernacles in those days. Our garments were white Feast Dresses that had been ordered from Jean Mabry's Benote Zion Dance School and Bezalel School of Dance. They had purple sashes and looked glorious. We were a Davidic Dance company and listened largely to music by Paul Wilbur, Barry and Batya Segal, and other Messianic Worship leaders of the time. The dance steps were Hebraic and were danced in a Machol (circle dance).

During the NLDN conference, my horizon was expanded as never before. I had no idea that there was a world of Praise and Worship Dance with Pageantry and Flags, and I was in awe the entire time. A few of my team members were present, and we took it all in with great wonder and curiosity. Where was God taking us with all of this? There were teams from Ohio, New York, and other States who were quite skillful. There were solo dancers as well as group dancers. One solo dancer ministered to me in such a way that I could not stop crying. It was a handsome, young, male dancer from New York, who danced to "I Can Only Imagine." I was taken inside the message of the song to such depth that I decided that I needed to get some training for this kind of dance. He was followed by a young lady who danced to "The Alabaster Box," another song that touched my heart deeply. I saw myself dancing before the Lord.

Dr. Pamela visited my table of jewelry that was on display in the foyer during the break. I got to talk with her for a short while, and she shared that she lived in Columbus, Ohio, and was about to launch a dance school with the Alpha class starting in October. This school was to be named the Eagles International Training Institute (EITI). My team members and I left this dance conference on a high note, and I don't think our wheels touched the ground as we drove back home to San Antonio. We knew that this was a new beginning for us.

The words from Dr. Pamela resonated in me, so in the following year, I traveled to Ohio for the Eagles International Training Institute's first summit and graduation. I met some of the students from the Alpha class on a shuttle bus from the airport to the hotel, and I asked them what class had been like and whether the skills they had learned opened new doors for them. Everyone was excited and a little nervous about their upcoming final exams. They all said that a new world had opened to them, and they encouraged me to enroll. I met people from various parts of the United States as well as some students from Mexico, Puerto Rico, and other places in the Caribbean islands. Wow! They exhibited their cultures in the dances they ministered, and I was just in awe.

I had a jewelry table there at the conference and a few anointing oils and gifts from the Holy Land, and I attended the night sessions. The atmosphere of the worship was on such an incredibly high level that I had never experienced, and I soaked it all in so deeply. I left the conference so transformed and prayed about what God wanted me to do.

It was not until 2008 that God allowed me to enroll in Dance Year 1. The year of study was intense, and I had to really manage my time as a wife, mother of four, grandmother, business owner, Bible teacher, dance director, and now student. The demands were high and, on another level, altogether. By the end of the semester, I had received a new revelation of biblical understanding about the art of praise and worship dance, and it excited me to pass on my newly gained knowledge to my team. We were growing together in a whole new way.

Unfortunately, the doors at my church did not open as I had hoped, and the lack of understanding what we were all about caused a rift between the choir director and me. He felt we were a distraction and used his influence with our pastor to keep us contained. We were only allowed to dance during the Praise and Worship services on first Sunday nights, and that was with certain restrictions. The annual Feast of Tabernacles was our highlight, as we could really dance there to our hearts' content in the festival grounds. The people loved us! We were free to put our own program together, and our garments were very colorful as we had been exposed to the Bezalel craft of Waves of Glory and the garments that preached a message on their own.

Summit Graduation in 2009 was my time to shine at the EITI. I loved the fact that we got to minister a dance as a graduating class, and it was exciting to think that this would be done in front of all teachers, students, and guests. I met so many wonderful students who had gone through the online classes with me, but we were now meeting face-to-face. One couple stood out to me, and we forged a very beautiful bond of love that still holds to this day. I prophesied over them that they were appointed by the Almighty to be the doorkeepers of the south. They live in South Africa on the most southern tip of the continent. God showed me keys they were given, and I gave them a prayer shawl with the prophetic utterance. My husband and some of my team members have since traveled there four times for conferences hosted by Apostles Neil and Philider Oortman (see graduating photo: last row fifth from the right is Philider, and her husband Neil a little under her on the row below). We even conducted a Night to Honor Israel there for two consecutive years with the Jewish Community in attendance.

Africa seemed to be the continent of God's choice to send us to. My husband and I received an invitation to come to Nigeria to attend the "Holy Ghost" conference hosted by Dr. Adejare Adeboye, the General Overseer of the Redeemed Churches of Christ, of which there are something like 8,000 around the world. We traveled to Redemption Camp, and on the way out of the airport, we met Dr. Myles Monroe, who was there as guest speaker along with our pastor, Dr. John Hagee. My dancers also accompanied us, and we were so honored to be given a space to minister a dance on the last day of the conference, where four million people were assembled. I had to pinch myself to see if this was not a dream. This was an outdoor stadium that took a jeep 20 minutes to drive its length. Incredible!!!! It was in December of 2009, and the heat and humidity were almost unbearable for us spoiled Westerners. They provided lodging for us in a hotel-like structure, and we received our food there as well. Under the stage, there were air-conditioned rooms provided for the foreign visitors, where we could go from time to time to refresh and get some snacks and drinks. It was there that we met Ron Kenoly, who was also a guest performer for this conference. My husband was a guest musician who ministered on the saxophone before they called up our pastor to speak. It was an exciting time, and I realized that the Apostolic Mantle rested on us.

As I continued with the EITI and enrolled in several courses, I received a mandate from Adonai to put together a Torah curriculum. I had found out in 1995 that I had Jewish ancestry on my mother's side and took a deep dive into my heritage that had been kept quiet for an obvious reason: the Holocaust.

Now the Lord wanted me to teach my new knowledge and the connections I had made to my Hebraic roots to the Church. I presented it to Apostle Pamela, who consulted with Messianic Rabbi Yisrael Ben Avraham of Etz Chaim Ministries in Austin. He looked over the curriculum and approved it.

I was beyond excited. The Apostolic Mantle had fallen on me. New doors began to open. The first Torah class formed, and I kept on writing new curricula. We are now offering Torah Years 1-4, as they developed over time.

One by one, my dance team members began to enroll in EITI courses. Some for dance, some for prophecy, some for Torah. We formed a TEN site and began teaching our community church dance teams, ever growing and ever learning more. God multiplied our numbers.

I received several opportunities to travel as a representative of the EITI, once again to Jos Nigeria in the Plateau State. The EITI's School of David Instructor Apostle Daps Gwom hosted the Feast of Incense conference, and some of the EITI's dancers joined me there along with my husband, who was also invited to minister on his instrument.

Apostle Pamela met us in South Africa, I was with her in Belize and Mexico on various occasions and got to be part of the travel ministry team. I learned so much from just being around her. She exudes love wherever she goes. She can also demand discipline in a stern but loving way. Without discipline, a team would not be very effective.

I learned this from her and apply it to my own team. Sometimes we are stretched physically and mentally, but it is for the Kingdom of God, and we know it will bring the desired harvest.

We have opened the Faith Apostoli Center here in our city so that the Eagles and TENs have a place to come, be trained, have fellowship, and experience the "family" connection we have in our great organization. This is the Heart of God, we know! We are MOVING FORWARD TOGETHER!!

ABOUT THE AUTHOR

Renate McWright, originally from Innsbruck, Austria, encountered Christ in 1977 at a Watchnight service, transforming her life. In 1996, she discovered her hidden Jewish ancestry and now passionately teaches the richness of Jewish roots and culture, honoring her heritage and faith journey alongside her husband, Tim, a former American soldier

RUNNING WITH THE HORSES - LEARN TO T.A.P. AND GO HIGHER

"If you have raced with men on foot and they have worn you out, how can you compete with horses? If you stumble in safe country, how will you manage in the thickets by the Jordan?" (Jeremiah 12:5 NIV).

Ministry is not for the faint of heart. Anyone who says "y.e.s." (yield, elevate, soar) to the call of God will face moments of pure exhaustion, discouragement, and even temptation to throw in the towel—more so in the lives of married couples in ministry. The weight of responsibility and accountability that comes with the shepherding and discipleship of God's people is enormous. Managing a household, ensuring your cup remains full through personal prayer and worship, and staying unified in marriage may feel unbearable. When ministry couples learn to "t.a.p. (tarry, align, pivot) in," they go higher and receive endurance to "run with horses."

God's call is not to survive ministry but to thrive in it. Jeremiah 12:5 serves as a reflection: If you are exhausted by the lesser battles, how will you handle the greater ones? God never intended for us to run in our own strength. Just as the eagle soars on and with the current of the wind, not by flapping its wings tirelessly, we are called to lean into the supernatural empowerment of the Holy Spirit.

Every couple in ministry or great leader faces this crossroads at some point in their faith journey—the choice between settling in weariness or pressing into God's greater strength. It is in this moment where we either succumb to stagnation or recognize the important need for transition and move forward. To run with footmen is to operate within your own limited human strength and abilities. However, running with horses requires supernatural empowerment from the Holy Spirit (see Zechariah 4:6 TLB), allowing you to develop spiritual fortitude.

Jeremiah 12:5 reminds us that greater assignments require greater endurance, but what happens when two are running together? We have been running this race side by side for nearly 36 years. We met as teenagers in high school, full of love and passion but with different levels of maturity and expectations, and a limited, inexperienced view on life. What worked for us then—our communication, our conflict resolution, our ways of showing and receiving love—does not always work for us now in our 50s. We have had to learn how to grow, mature, and adapt, together and individually. One of the most delicate challenges in marriage, especially in ministry, is learning to remain yoked and harnessed (more on this concept later) to God's purpose and calling. It is important to understand that, as a couple, you will not always grow at the same pace or in the same direction. It is during these times when conflict and disagreement are highest and submitting to God and one another is most required (Ephesians 5:21). But there is still unity in fulfilling purpose together. We have learned that staying in rhythm requires managing our expectations of each other and refusing to become stuck in old patterns that no longer serve us. The expression of our call may differ, and our needs may change over time, but choosing to meet each other in those changes with grace and humility keeps us strong. Running with the horses does not mean you always *feel* in sync; on the contrary, it means you've committed to keep running, adjusting, and trusting God, who called you both to run together.

God allows certain challenges to come our way to strengthen our faith, build our character, mature us, and prepare us for the next level. James 1:2-4 reinforces this by encouraging us to remain joyful and persevere. Greater responsibility requires greater and more strenuous testing and proving. Yet, through it all, God's consistency remains. Through our obedience, we are assured of His deliverance.

For couples in ministry, life's challenges are real, but they do not define you. They will not overtake you. As long as you remain aligned with God, you will overcome. Greater responsibility demands greater endurance. Luke 12:48 (NIV) reminds us: *"From everyone who has been given much, much will be demanded; and from the one who has been entrusted with much, much more will be asked."* Learning to "t.a.p. in" can be the difference maker between quitting and elevating.

T.A.P. In

As kids, we watched the World Wrestling Federation (WWF) matches on television. One of the more exciting matchups would involve two favorite wrestlers joining forces in a tag-team bout against another team. The rules were simple:

1. Only one team member is allowed in the ring at a time.
2. The partner must wait patiently outside the ring and be "tapped in" to switch in and become legally eligible to wrestle.

Depending on who you were rooting for, this could be exhilarating or excruciating to watch. Here is the notable key—*the team that learned to manage the "tap-in" could control the outcome.* Selah! The "tap-in" allows the partner to rest, refresh, or renew while the other partner wears down the opponent. The key to victory is found in one team's ability to successfully prevent the opponent from reaching his corner to "tap in" his partner, who is waiting with renewed strength to enter the fight. The strategy is to keep the battle to a two-on-one matchup until the diminished opponent is successfully pinned for a count of three. So, what's the point? *The one who stays refreshed wins!* Having renewed strength means that you must embrace the process of accessing, possessing, and harnessing God's best for you and your partner by learning to t.a.p.

Winning battles or running with the horses requires a commitment to and a longing for the deep things in God. There are at least three keys needed to t.a.p. into next-level, next-dimension momentum:

- Tarry
- Align
- Pivot

Tarry-Learning to Sit Before You Soar

Tarrying is often associated with waiting or remaining fixed in a location until the appointed passage of time is completed. But a more profound revelation of this principle requires laying down (submitting or surrendering) our will for His, regardless of what is said, done, and—more importantly—how we feel in the middle of it. It is about obediently serving while the Father reveals His plan for us in preparation to release us into His next assignment for our lives. January 2017 was one of those moments. I (Lawrence) ministered from the book of Joel 2:4. The title of the message was "It's Time to Run." After releasing that word, I began experiencing unexplained migraines in the workplace that would ultimately lead to an unplanned and untimely resignation from a six-figure job.

There was no plan, no savings—nothing. This would mark the beginning of leaning into the tarry. For two years, we remained in a place of humble yet faithful uncertainty. During that time, we launched Ambassadors Academy. Running, right? In 2019, we experienced even more significant setbacks in our family, finances, school, and overall ministry. We lost ministry leaders;

we lost the building facility; our home was in foreclosure; we experienced significant attacks against our family spiritually, mentally, emotionally, and physically. Every pillar of the vision God gave us at that time—faith, family, fellowship, fitness (emotional, mental, physical, and financial), was falling apart. And, like most leaders, we dug in, plowed ahead, and pressed forward—we kept running with the footmen. We had a "no matter what" determination, but God had other plans. He was increasing our stamina to run with the horses. God mandated a sabbatical—in other words, a time to sit, reflect, adjust, and receive (tarry) without the distractions of demand or responsibility. We often miss God's best because we are worn out (and become burned out) by the busyness of the assignment (albeit noble and well-intentioned) instead of being aligned with the purpose and will of Adonai.

Table Talk: Let's pause and unpack this together:

1. In what areas of our lives or ministry have we been running ahead of God instead of sitting and waiting for His instruction together?

2. How have we responded to seasons of forced stillness or loss—and what might God be trying to reveal to us in the waiting?

Align-Yoked to God; Harnessed Together

Alignment (agreement) is the process of getting in line with His perfect plan. For ministry couples, this resembles two concepts:

- Yoked like oxen (vertical relationship with God): Matthew 11:29.

- Harnessed like horses (horizontal relationship with spouse): Jeremiah 46:4.

Yokes are for preparation and learning for burden-bearing, while harnesses are for strength, readiness, partnership, and coordinated action. A yoke is about learning to align with God's will and pace. A harness is about aligning with your partner for warfare, battle, and movement!

The Greek word for "alignment" in the Bible is *katartismos*, meaning "to properly align, to set in original order, or to put a thing in its proper position." When spiritually aligned, you are in sync with your calling, live authentically, and experience clarity and purpose through the Holy Spirit. Spiritual alignment requires surrendering your will to God's will, listening to His voice, and allowing the Holy Spirit to lead. When we live in alignment, we experience peace, fulfillment, and direction because we walk in step with our divine assignment. However, distractions and weariness can pull us out of alignment. In Jeremiah 12, the prophet becomes consumed with everything around him. He steps into the dangerous territory of comparison, questioning why God allows injustices to persist. God's response is direct: "If you are concerned about this, how in the world will you handle the greater challenges ahead?" In other words, "Take your eyes off the things of this world, and set them on Me."

Table Talk: Let's pause and unpack this together:

1. Are we truly yoked to Christ in our personal spiritual lives—and how is that impacting our ability to move in unity as a couple?

2. Where are we possibly out of alignment with each other, and what adjustments do we need to make to walk in step with both God and one another?

Pivot-Obedience in Transition

Pivoting requires moving (faith to faith—elevation) from old plans to His new blueprint in obedience. Sometimes, God calls us to pivot, to step out in faith and transition from old patterns to His new blueprint. Pivoting requires obedience. It demands that we leave behind our comfort zones and move from faith to faith, from glory to glory (Romans 1:17; 2 Corinthians 3:18).

Jeremiah had to pivot his perspective. He was focused on external injustices, but God redirected him to see the bigger picture—His divine process of strengthening and proving His people. Likewise, couples in ministry must learn to pivot from frustration to faith, from striving to surrender, from self-sufficiency to supernatural reliance.

God allows challenges not to break us but to prepare us. The footmen—the daily struggles, disappointments, and pressures—are part of the process of refining us for greater responsibilities. When we Tarry, Align, and Pivot, we will not only keep up but will also run with the horses.

Table Talk: Let's pause and unpack this together:

1. What old patterns or comforts are we being called to release in order to obey God's new direction for our marriage and ministry?

2. Are we resisting a necessary pivot because of fear or fatigue, and how can we encourage one another to trust God in the shift?

Going Higher

Ministry is not just about stepping into a role; it is about embracing the weight and responsibility that come with the call. When you say "yes" to God, you must also say "yes" to the refining process, the trials, and the sacrifices required to steward His anointing well. The anointing is costly, and it demands everything. It is not given lightly, and it is not sustained through human effort alone. It requires surrender, perseverance, and a supernatural grace to endure.

Jesus warned in Luke 14:28-30 that anyone who desires to build must first count the cost. This is the reality of answering the call. The weight of the anointing will stretch you, test you, and press you beyond what you think you can bear. But when you learn to carry it with grace, leaning on the Holy Spirit rather than your own strength, you will find yourself not just surviving but soaring.

The call to run with the horses is not for the faint of heart. It is for those who are willing to be shaped by fire, refined by trials, and strengthened by God's presence. To whom much is given, much is required. Yet, the same God who calls you will sustain you. When you learn to Tarry in His presence, Align with His will, and Pivot in obedience, you will not be crushed by the weight; you will be empowered by it.

So, run with grace. Run with endurance. Run with the confidence that God has anointed and equipped you for this journey. And when the road feels overwhelming, remember this: The weight you carry is not a burden; instead, it is a mark of His trust in you.

A Closing Prayer for Couples in Ministry:

> *Father, thank You for the call to run—not just with footmen, but with horses. Thank You for trusting us with the weight of Your glory and the responsibility of leadership. We surrender our will, our plans, and our pace to You. Teach us to Tarry in Your presence, Align with Your purpose, and Pivot with grace when You shift us. Strengthen our marriage and ministry. Help us to see each other not just as partners but as purpose-filled vessels chosen to run together. Let our love be rooted in You and refreshed by You. May we not grow weary in well-doing, but let us be renewed daily by Your Spirit. In Jesus' name, Amen.*

Couples Interactive Elevation Activity

Sit together and discuss one area where you feel out of rhythm—emotionally, spiritually, or physically. Identify one step to restore unity. Then, share what "running with the horses" looks like in this season and one place you need God's supernatural strength. Now, face each other, hold hands, and take a moment to breathe and be present. One at a time, share:

1. Where do you feel most connected right now?
2. Where do you feel a disconnect—in heart, spirit, or purpose?

Now, speak one affirmation over your spouse and one prayer request. Close by praying aloud for each other's strength and for unity, as He realigns you to be empowered as one.

ABOUT THE AUTHORS

Apostles Lawrence and Tamara Nichols are visionary leaders, authors, and certified Maxwell coaches dedicated to equipping transformational leaders in ministry, business, and education. Cofounders of KAATC and Ambassadors Academy, they provide leadership and discipleship training while passionately serving as mentors, educators, and servant leaders advancing lasting Kingdom impact.

MY WORSHIP IS FOR REAL

Yvonne Payne

A Wilderness Walk: The Testimony of Obedience and Healing

My wilderness experience has been marked by both spiritual and physical battles. For nearly ten years, I've attended the EITI Summit—a place of refreshing and alignment for prophetic artists. But most years, I barely made it. Finances were tight. My schedule was stretched. At times, it felt like everything was against me making it to the summit. Yet, God saw fit to make a way every time. Whether through unexpected provision or divine favor, He carried me through. Every trip to the summit was a prophetic declaration: I'm still standing, and I'm still worshipping.

Another part of my wilderness has been living with edema—a chronic illness where my body swells throughout the day, sometimes to the point where walking becomes nearly impossible. The discomfort has been severe, affecting not only my physical body but also my emotional and spiritual strength. Some days, I cried out in frustration and weakness, asking God why I had to endure this.

But even in my pain, I've danced. Even in my weakness, I've worshipped. The Lord met me in worship—He strengthened me in ways no medication could. Through every worship session, every act of faith, every movement of my body, God infused me with His strength. His Word in Isaiah 40:29 (NIV) became my anchor: *"He gives strength to the weary and increases the power of the weak."* He is real in my soul. My worship is not for performance—it is survival. It is intimacy. It is warfare. It is healing.

The Heart of Worship

Worship is not about music alone. It's about the posture of the heart. John 4:24 (NKJV) reminds us, *"God is Spirit, and those who worship Him must worship in spirit and truth."* Worship is not confined to church walls, perfect voices, or choreographed routines. It is the sound of surrender. It is the song of the heart that has seen pain but chooses praise. It is the movement of someone who has nothing left but their faith.

True worship flows from the depths of our soul—especially in seasons of wilderness. It is easy to lift our hands when life is good, but real worship happens when you have every reason to quit, yet you bow low and say, "Nevertheless, You are still worthy, Lord."

When Jesus was tested in the wilderness (Matthew 4:1-11 NIV), He responded to every temptation with the Word. His worship wasn't in what He said alone—it was in what He *didn't* do. He didn't bow to comfort. He didn't compromise for a shortcut.

He held firm to His identity, trusting in God's provision and purpose. That is worship. And that is what God desires from us.

Understanding Wilderness: A Place of Refinement

The wilderness is not punishment—it is preparation. It's the place where we are stripped of distractions, where the noise of the world quiets down, and where God's voice becomes clearer. Just as the Israelites wandered in the wilderness before entering the Promised Land, so must we walk through seasons of testing before stepping into our destiny.

But the wilderness isn't just about waiting—it's about *becoming*. In Deuteronomy 8:2-3 (NIV), God tells Israel, *"Remember how the Lord your God led you all the way in the wilderness ... to humble and test you in order to know what was in your heart."* The same is true for us. The wilderness reveals who we really are and, more importantly, who God really is.

The Israelites often doubted, complained, and rebelled, yet God remained faithful. He gave manna from heaven, water from rocks, and a cloud by day and fire by night. He was near. And in your wilderness, He is near too.

Worship as Warfare: Dance and Song That Break Chains

In my own life, worship through dance has become a weapon. I've ministered with aching feet and swollen legs. I've danced when I could barely stand. And in those moments, the Spirit of God would show up like a mighty rushing wind.

David danced before the Lord with all his might, even when others looked down on him (2 Samuel 6:14-16 NIV). His dance was not for man—it was for the God who delivered him. Likewise, my dance is not performance—it is prophetic. It shifts atmospheres. It invites the presence of God.

Worship songs have carried me through nights of pain and silence. When words failed me, worship spoke for me. In Acts 16, Paul and Silas worshipped in prison—and chains broke. The same still happens today. Worship isn't just expression—it is breakthrough. Worship breaks through the darkness. Worship breaks through pain. Worship breaks through fear.

The Promised Land: Stepping Into Destiny

After forty years of wandering, the Israelites finally entered the Promised Land. But it took faith, obedience, and unwavering trust in God's promises. Likewise, every believer has a destiny—a place God has promised—but the path there is paved through worship, obedience, and perseverance.

God rewrites our stories. What looked like defeat becomes destiny. What was meant to harm us, God uses for good (Genesis 50:20 NIV). I am not defined by illness, lack, or delay. I am defined by God's promises, His anointing, and His purpose for me.

I may have started in a small church in Boston, but I now dance and minister with prophetic power. I may have been weak in my body, but I am strong in the Spirit. My life testifies that God rewrites stories—and He will rewrite yours too.

Soaring as Eagles: Rising Above Every Obstacle

Isaiah 40:31 (NIV) declares, *"But those who hope in the Lord will renew their strength. They will soar on wings like eagles; they will run and not grow weary, they will walk and not be faint."* Eagles do not run from storms—they rise above them. They use the winds meant to destroy them as fuel to fly higher.

This is the prophetic picture of the believer who worships in the wilderness. We don't deny the storm, but we rise above it. Through worship, we are strengthened to walk through valleys and climb mountains. Through worship, we learn to soar.

TEN Worldwide and the Eagles International Training Institute have taught me to worship with wisdom, patience, character, obedience, prayer, thanksgiving, and long-suffering. These are not just virtues—they are tools. Tools to survive the wilderness. Tools to soar above the storm. Tools to reach the promise.

Our call is not to remain grounded in fear but to fly in faith. We are called to serve with humility and soar in excellence. That is the heart of the eagle. That is the life of a worshipper.

Forgiveness in the Wilderness: A Path to True Worship

In my wilderness journey, I've learned that forgiveness is essential. Offenses are inevitable, but choosing forgiveness over offense keeps our hearts pure and receptive to God's Word. The EITI taught me that forgiveness is better than the offense—it maintains a clean heart, ready for divine revelation.

Forgiveness is a deliberate choice that is not based on feelings. It's a supernatural act that prevents bitterness from taking root. As we know forgiveness is a choice of the will, it isn't a matter of feelings; it's a matter of the heart. Unforgiveness hinders spiritual growth and blocks the flow of God's blessings. Embracing forgiveness aligns us with God's mercy, fostering a closer relationship with Him.

The Power of Prayer: My Lifeline to Destiny

One of the greatest weapons God gave me in the wilderness was prayer. When I couldn't dance, I prayed. When I couldn't walk, I whispered His name. When I had no words left, I cried out from the depths of my spirit. Prayer became not just communication—it became my lifeline.

Prayer took me from pain to purpose. It bridged the gap between desperation and destiny. It realigned my focus, renewed my strength, and kept me grounded in truth when my emotions told me otherwise. Prayer reminded me of who I am and, more importantly, who God is.

Romans 12:12 (NIV) encourages us to *"Be joyful in hope, patient in affliction, faithful in prayer."* Faithful prayer kept my heart open during seasons of silence and confusion. It kept me anchored to the One who sees beyond the wilderness into the Promised Land.

Prayer is a form of worship. It's a posture of humility and surrender. Every time we bow our hearts or lift our hands, we declare that He is sovereign. Prayer transforms us from the inside out—it's the place where I encountered God not as a distant deity but as Abba, my Father, my Defender, and my Friend.

In the EITI, I learned that prophetic intercession is not just a ministry—it's a mantle. When I stood in prayer, I stood in my identity. And as I prayed for others, I often found healing for myself. Prayer was not just the key to my next level—it was the vehicle that carried me through the desert and into destiny.

My Worship Is For Real

This journey—through dance, pain, testing, and breakthrough—has shown me that worship is my anchor. It is how I fight. It is how I overcome. It is how I hear God. Whether I'm in the valley or on the mountain, I will worship.

My worship is not rehearsed. It is real. It has been born in tears, strengthened in fire, and released in praise. I know God is real—not just because I've read the Bible, but because I've seen Him heal me. I've watched Him provide. I've heard Him speak. He is in my soul. He is the breath in my lungs.

If you're in the wilderness today, don't give up. Worship. Dance. Sing. Cry. But don't stop worshipping. Your promise is on the other side of your praise. Your healing is in the sound of your surrender.

Reflection Questions

1. What is your current wilderness, and how might God be using it to refine your faith?
2. In what ways has worship become a lifeline for you during seasons of pain or uncertainty?
3. How do you express worship beyond music—through dance, service, obedience, or prayer?
4. What obstacles are keeping you from soaring, and how can you surrender them to God?
5. Are you allowing God to rewrite your story, or are you still holding on to old chapters?

Final Words

You are not alone in your journey. Whether you're battling illness, fighting to trust, or learning to worship through tears—know this: God is with you. And your worship is not wasted. It is seen. It is powerful. It is for real.

Personal Assignment: A Journey Into True Worship

As you've read through this reflection on worship, healing, and destiny, now it's your turn to respond. Worship is not just something we do—it's who we are. It flows from a life fully surrendered to the Father.

Take time this week to walk through the following True Worship Assignment. Don't rush. Let the Holy Spirit guide you.

1. Set a Dedicated Time of Worship (Minimum 30 Minutes)
   - Find a quiet space—just you and God.
   - No distractions. Turn off your phone. Light a candle if it helps you focus.
   - Play worship music that helps you connect with God or sit in silence.
   - Begin by thanking God, not for what He's done but for who He is.
2. Dance or Move as an Offering
   - Let your body respond to God's presence.
   - Even if you're not a trained dancer, offer your movements to Him.
   - Don't worry about how it looks—just move in freedom.
   - Let this be a physical expression of "Here I am, Lord."
3. Write a Personal Worship Letter to the Father
   - Pour out your heart on paper or in a journal.
   - Tell Him what you've been through and how you see Him in your story.

Include:
- Where you feel you're in the "wilderness"
- What you believe He's preparing you for
- One area where you're choosing forgiveness over offense
- One promise you're holding on to

4. Pray Boldly Over Your Destiny
   - Speak life over your future.
   - Ask God to remove anything blocking your worship (bitterness, fear, offense).
   - Invite Him to rewrite your story.
   - Declare aloud: *"Father, my worship is for real. You are worthy, no matter what."*

5. Reflect With Scripture

   Meditate on these verses during the week:
   - John 4:23-24 – Worship in spirit and in truth
   - Psalm 51:17 – A broken and contrite heart
   - Isaiah 40:31 – Soaring on wings like eagles
   - Romans 12:1 – Offer your body as a living sacrifice
   - Deuteronomy 8:2-3 – The purpose of the wilderness

Closing Challenge

At the end of the week, ask yourself:
- Has my definition of worship changed?
- Am I ready to worship in every season?
- Will I give God my whole heart, not just my song?

Then, write a short one-paragraph declaration beginning with:

"My worship is for real because …"

Let this be your altar, your offering, your promise.

May God be with you every step of the way.

Yvonne Payne

ABOUT THE AUTHOR

Born and raised in Boston, I worship at Concord Baptist Church under Rev. Dr. Conley Hughes Jr. My passion for worship through dance led me to TEN Worldwide and Eagles International Training Institute. Through trials and growth, worship has become my weapon, my calling, and my testimony of God's enduring faithfulness.

THE MOUTH SPEAKS

*"She speaks with wisdom,
and faithful instruction is on her tongue."*

(Proverbs 31:26 NIV)

According to Robert K. Dellenbach, "When you open your mouth to speak, you reveal a great deal. The words you use and your speaking are like a blueprint of who you are deep inside ..."

Without a solid grasp of your identity in Christ, you might become susceptible to the opinions and influences of others. Our identity is rooted in Christ. How are we rooted in Christ? Through an intimate relationship with the Father. You might feel that your voice is insignificant, leading you to remain silent as a new believer. Your primary desire is to please God, and He places individuals in your life to guide, teach, and prepare you for His Kingdom's work. When God empowers His children, their true identities emerge, showcasing the distinct purpose He has assigned to them. What unique purpose has God entrusted to you that calls for you to express yourself vocally? The influence of our voice can shape the spaces we live in and the lives we affect. Our voice can build and equip the church, which means to edify the body through the gifts He has given us (Ephesians 4:12). Failing to communicate our thoughts and feelings endangers both our own lives and the lives of those around us. We must embrace the power and authority bestowed upon us to speak into the lives of others, creating meaningful change. We strive to use our voice to create connections and promote understanding. The spoken words have the power to shape our relationships and society, and we want to use them wisely. Our mission is to travel to nations and share the gospel (Mark 16:15); a silent approach will not fulfill that purpose.

My journey began in 1996, when I committed my life to Christ. I felt a void, realizing that being a believer encompassed more than just attending church, teaching Sunday school, and leading a dance ministry at my local congregation. I struggled to understand my identity in Christ and battled with low self-esteem, often listening to negative thoughts that contradicted God's truth. The saying, "An idle mind is the devil's playground" resonates deeply, especially during youth when confusion clouds your thoughts. It's easy to internalize the words spoken over you, whether by yourself or others. It's crucial to affirm yourself when no one else is present. Surrounding ourselves with spiritually mature individuals is essential. For me, The Eagles Network (TEN) and Eagles International Training Institute (EITI) have been pivotal in this journey. The impact on everyone I met—from the TEN staff to the instructors and administrators at the EITI—has been profound.

The EITI and TEN provided the education and training I obtained. God placed this institute in my path to enhance my ability to communicate confidently. I am grateful to God for the church member who introduced me to TEN and the EITI in 2010. Since then, I have maintained a connection with the EITI and TEN. Initially, when I joined TEN, I was utterly reserved about spiritual topics, feeling I had little to contribute and often preferring to listen and learn. I often feel a deep sense of doubt and worry when I consider opening up to others. What if they don't understand? What if they judge me? These thoughts create a heavy burden on my heart. I often wonder if I am good enough to share what God put on my heart. You might not always know the following steps or feel you are the right person to share what God has given you. This is where God intervenes, providing for your journey.

Trust in the Father throughout this process. Allowing Him to influence your thoughts and speech is significant. I often compared myself to Moses, who struggled with speaking. I experienced doubt regarding how to articulate my thoughts or convey my feelings while serving others and embracing the calling that God has given me. In Exodus 4:10 (NIV), Moses expressed, *"Pardon your servant, Lord. I have never been eloquent, neither in the past nor since you have spoken to your servant. I am slow of speech and tongue."* When God calls you to speak, He will provide the words you need. These words are meant to uplift others, not to bring them down. God will guide us in using our voice for His Kingdom, equipping us to speak into our areas of influence (Isaiah 58:1). Individuals were appointed to assist me in realizing the vision that God had bestowed upon me. These may seem like minor blessings, yet they represent significant milestones in the various seasons of my life. When I helped others, I was not seeking recognition. When you are in prayer, asking the Lord to enlarge your territory and to use you when He needs you, be prepared. I was so busy being an instrument for God that I did not think about the impact it would have on others. When we are busy doing the work of the Father, we do not think about ourselves (1 Corinthians 15:58). Doing the work of the Father is using your voice.

It has been six years since the Holy Spirit urged me to share my story. Sharing my story means finding my voice. My initial response was disbelief: "You want me to do what?" I struggled with writing my book, *Breaking the Shackles of Unforgiveness*. I felt embarrassed about revealing the events of my life. I worried about others' opinions and reactions. I know I'm not alone in this experience. Often, we endure challenges for the sake of others. Everyone has a story to tell. My narrative has the potential to aid others in their healing journey. True healing requires digging deep; it's not just about surface-level fixes. I discover more about myself in my writing. Through sharing my story, I aim to demonstrate to others that they are not isolated in their experiences. They, too, have a voice. Our stories are meant for those we connect with, impacting lives through words. Being obedient to the Father by using our voice inspires others to do the same. No one else can tell your story. I often ask God, "Why me?" and the response I receive is, "Why not you? I have been preparing you for this moment."

The key focus for me is to become the best version of myself. I deserve freedom, and so do you. The initial step on my journey to freedom involved keeping an open mind, which enabled God to operate within me. Next, I needed to stay connected to the

Father through His word and prayer. Finally, I had to follow the guidance that God provided me. When you embrace spiritual and emotional freedom, restoration and deliverance naturally follow. Throughout this journey, I have rediscovered my identity. I no longer see myself as just an individual. For instance, I stood in front of the mirror and asked myself, "Stephanie, who are you without your voice?" Embracing an open mind is crucial for allowing God to shape your life. When you let your faith illuminate your path, you will better understand your true self. You discover clarity and confidence by placing your trust in a higher power. It wasn't an overnight transformation, and I'm still on my journey, but I have made significant progress.

To discover your life's purpose, it's crucial to participate in activities that deepen your insight. God is constantly reaching out to us; we need to be in a place where we can receive His messages. There are specific blueprints designed for our lives—plans meant for us to follow. Each individual has one, and we must align ourselves with God's will to access His guidance. I recognize a plan of action is in place, but I occasionally doubt my preparedness to follow through. Throughout the years, I have committed to personal growth by acquiring new skills and refining my existing talents. This is where the EITI has played a significant role. The institute has also helped me cultivate my spiritual gifts. Through the training, resources, and support I have received, I have cultivated my distinct voice. Anything valuable requires investment, enabling you to evolve into a better version of yourself. Our voice is not the only impact we have on others. It is using our voice to execute what is given to us. This is what the Institute has shown me over the years. Actions speak louder than words.

In summary, you are not intended to navigate the plan by yourself. There will be others who will support you throughout your journey. Given your skills and resources, it is crucial to execute the plan that has been entrusted to you. When God provides a vision, He also equips you with the means to achieve it. Have faith in the journey. I had to embrace that faith myself. For a long time, I recognized that God had appointed me to a particular position within the fivefold ministry. His message was unmistakable. Yet, I chose to flee. I ran because I struggled to envision myself using my voice for God's Kingdom. I felt inadequate, believing I lacked the words to impact others positively. However, if you run for too long, exhaustion sets in. Eventually, you reach a point where running is no longer viable. I had to yield to the process. My mindset shifted from "No, I can't" to "Yes, I will take a step forward and trust You to guide me, Father." Even if I had to face my fears, I moved forward into my next chapter.

What lies ahead for you? Rest assured that you are not alone. Before fully committing to your journey, seeking God's direction to uncover any obstacles preventing you from achieving His purpose is crucial. During this season, God requires us to be open and willing vessels. You may encounter discouragement as the enemy seeks to thwart your success. The enemy has already glimpsed your potential. Your growth is not solely for your benefit; it serves those you are meant to reach. Those connected to you will gain from the vision entrusted to you. In my experience, this is clear: Every course and training I've undertaken has equipped me to express the voice God has given me. The only limits we face are the ones we impose on ourselves.

You've attempted to navigate life on your terms. It's time to release control and allow God to take charge. Embrace self-love deeply enough to explore the hidden aspects of your being. Permit God to elevate you to the person He intended you to be. Stay true to yourself and avoid comparing your journey to others, as each of us has a distinct path.

Reflection Questions:

1. What holds you back from expressing what God has called you to share?

2. What actions are you prepared to take to break the silence of your voice?

3. What are the hindrances that hold you back from your voice being heard?

ABOUT THE AUTHOR

Stephanie Vann is a licensed commission pastor and founder of Oasis Apostolic Training Center. She focuses on helping believers transition from traditional practices to a Kingdom-oriented lifestyle. Additionally, she wrote *Breaking the Shackles of Unforgiveness*, a book aimed at helping individuals who struggle with forgiveness, guiding them toward a life of wholeness.

BECOMING ME: A WORSHIP WARRIOR'S JOURNEY

"Who am I?" That question echoed in my heart as I transitioned from a lifetime of government and reserve military service into the unknown. What I didn't know then was that God was about to lead me into a journey of rediscovery through dance, worship, and a training institute that would change my life forever.

My journey with the Eagles International Training Institute (EITI) began in October 2013. I retired from my government job with thirty-three years of government service, and I retired from the Air Force Reserve in 1995 with fifteen years of service as a reservist. I was ready to teach, train, and mentor young dancers with the help of a team. I had the idea of creating my mobile dance school, Adore Him Dance School & Studio, and I prepared to embark on my teaching journey. To become an excellent teacher, a continual learning process is necessary to stay updated with new ideas and perspectives.

I was interested in a dance network that would allow me to learn more about my craft and connect with others who shared my passion for dance. I chose to study the course Dance Year 1 with Apostle Pamela Scott after discovering that one of my friends was a student in The Eagles Network Worldwide (TEN). It was too late for me to start with TEN because they were in the last module, preparing to graduate the TEN students. One of the dressmakers, who eventually made my dance garment, informed me about the EITI, which offered a more advanced training than TEN. After attending my friend's TEN graduation and researching this innovative training institute, I applied to participate in the EITI and was accepted. I was thrilled and excited to get accepted into this innovative dance program. At the time of my acceptance, the EITI offered dance as one of the major courses for which a graduate would receive a certificate. Dr. Scott provided the opportunity to obtain a dance license.

When I completed my dance course, Apostle Pamela Scott saw me as more than a dancer as I learned more about myself, the biblical foundation, and the study of dance. Apostle Pamela demonstrates her insight and spiritual discernment to all her students, enabling them to gain a deeper understanding of themselves under her guidance. The Discovering Our Spiritual Gifts and Talents assessment test is administered more than once, depending on your EITI course. With the help of the spiritual assessment test, discovering who you are becomes clearer. The spiritual assessment test could provide more spiritual information than you can imagine or see. Apostle Pamela sees further spiritually than we can know and tells us about our calling before we see the callings, talents, and abilities in the spiritual assessment test.

We often do not understand or recognize our spiritual gifts and talents, what they mean, or how to identify them. One way to discover the real you is to recognize the spiritual gifts and talents God has given you.

The journey of my first class in the EITI was life-transforming, and I quickly realized that I had so much more to offer beyond leading, dancing, teaching, or mentoring dancers. Each student who graduates is an Eagle. The identification of Eagle as a graduate of the EITI is prophetic and has an empowering message to soar to new heights for God, ourselves, and the nation. The EITI motto is to serve with humility and soar with excellence. Many have come to understand that our mission is not to outperform or compete with our brothers and sisters in Christ but to unite to take the nations for God. We move forward together. I saw the prophetic meaning of eagles and what eagles do. In learning about what eagles do, we begin to understand what we do as Eagles and why we do what we do. Apostle Pamela's heart is for the nations, and we, as Eagles, play an essential part in bringing the nations to God.

After completing my first course in the EITI, Dance Year 1, in 2014, I obtained a license in dance ministry and was now referred to as a dance minister; I had no idea that there was a specific name and position associated with it. Upon completing my Dance Year 1 course, I had the opportunity to teach in The Eagles Network (TEN) Worldwide in my city. TEN falls under the umbrella of the EITI, which was founded by Apostle Pamela Scott. The training consists of five modules designed to educate students on various topics. The topics and courses have grown over the years. TEN is exploding and now exists in many different nations. The purpose is to gather, train, equip, and educate those called and send them to our cities, regions, and countries. While I was a teacher in TEN, it was exciting to share the biblical foundation of dance and see the growth of many as they learned why they dance. I also learned about myself as I poured out to those who wanted to learn more about worship, dance, the biblical foundation of why we dance, and principles of Christ-like living to make a difference in their sphere of influence. Training and exposure to diverse people and groups tend to shift our mindsets and perspectives on those things within our influence to more excellent dimensions. All students are accountable for ensuring that their responsibilities are carried out under authority. No loose cannons exist in our camp or the camp we worship. The worship houses and places we are currently planted in are better because of the excellent training we received from the EITI or TEN training.

Maintaining a relationship with the EITI over the years, taking various courses, learning from different staff members and teachers, and networking with other Eagles can change how we view ourselves in the broader context of fulfilling the Great Commission. Our influence extends beyond our families, churches, regions, nations, and cities. The assignment is more significant than ourselves; it is a kingdom assignment. God's manifested presence is seen in us, bringing many to Him and establishing His kingdom on earth. We, as Eagles, serve and soar with excellence in our respective places or where we live. We preach, pray, prophesy, teach, intercede, lay hands on the sick, cast out demons, see people in their calling before they do, speak life to a dying world, and unite to bring many to Christ across the globe while seeing God as mighty and worthy of honor, love, and power.

As the EITI expanded its courses to include various forms of the arts, business, and theology, many, including myself, were impacted by the excellent training, which activated and equipped us to launch into our spheres of influence. The spiritual growth and EITI training over the last twelve years have been evident in those close to me. Sometimes, those who are not near me see the EITI training that can shed light on others. However, because of God's mercy, compassion, and love, many are drawn to God through the EITI training I have received. Matthew 5:16 (ESV) says, *"In the same way, let your light shine before others, so that they may see your good works and give glory to your Father who is in heaven."*

The real me has evolved and continues to grow as I learn and discover God's heart regarding those who desperately seek and thirst after him. Looking back to 2013, when I first started with the EITI, I see a different me and many spiritual changes in my life. My spiritual development and changes have drawn me closer to God's presence. I know that nothing I have done in my strength is worthy of mention. Philippians 2:13 (AMP) says, *"For it is [not your strength, but it is] God who is effectively at work in you, both to will and to work [that is, strengthening, energizing, and creating in you the longing and the ability to fulfill your purpose] for His good pleasure."*

Some discoveries about myself were complex and required spiritual revelation, which the Holy Spirit would provide me through EITI exposure and training. The hard places of my heart became the Holy places, where the Holy Spirit could reveal his purposes in my life. When the Holy Spirit directed me to the right courses, I received help from the instructors and students at the right time and in the right season. Despite how I saw myself, I needed to see who I was and who God created me to be for His service. The classes and curricula I have taken have opened and peeled back the layers of insecurities, drawing back into the shadows the fear of men's opinions that had bound me for many years. The Holy Spirit revealed Himself in the appropriate courses that fit my calling for this generation and the future. I am still learning and unfolding some things; the journey continues. But I am set to continue the spiritual journey that God has set me on. Understanding and connecting with those who want to pursue what God has for us is all worth the journey of discovering the real me. No matter what comes out of us, God has made the journey worthwhile.

Perseverance, endurance, patience, and learning to love the unlovely were all attributes that helped me become the real me. The EITI training and equipping are not intended to make me compete with my fellow brothers and sisters in Christ but to unite with them in bringing the harvest for His kingdom. We press toward the mark of the higher calling, not the calling of comparing ourselves to one another. We, as Eagles, serve with humility and soar with excellence. The perfecting of the saints is for the work of the ministry, not to brag about how many certificates we have or how beautiful our dance garments are.

It takes perseverance and endurance to complete a course of study. When we recognize the importance of our assignment and understand that God is with us, regardless of the situation, our eyes and minds will remain focused on completing the task at hand. In my case, there was a sense of stretching and discomfort in learning about the real me. Through the EITI training, it was easier to integrate and apply the learning experiences from the EITI courses by activating, sending, and equipping. During the integration process of implementing the lessons learned, I discovered that many people, although associated with their local assemblies, have no connection with like-minded individuals in advancing the kingdom of God. Many are locked into old mindsets and are unable to change their spheres of influence. As an EITI student, an opportunity to explore and discover your unknown is open for you to find, take hold of, and accept your calling.

The EITI annual worship summits are excellent avenues to enjoy the freedom only God brings through the indwelling praises of those who want to listen, hear, and obey His voice. My Dallas, Texas, cousins have attended for many years to support me in graduating from various classes. The first time I graduated from Dance Year 1 in 2014, my Texas aunt and one of my cousins were there to help me. They were so moved by the excitement, worship, and freedom of worship that they were glad to see I was a part of this worship experience. They left the summit happy that they could attend the worship and graduation.

Who is the real me? Only God knows, but He slowly reveals who I am in Him. My identity is more than my family's biological connection; it is about my spiritual connection with Him and the Christ-like character that I strive to develop with the Holy Spirit's help to serve others who need to know who they are in Him. The real me allows God to select the best people for me to connect with and to understand when to associate with the right tribe to experience the life journey that can sometimes seem rough and hard to continue. I am allowing God to tell me, correct me, and reveal to me as much as I can handle. Obedience to His voice is my desire to continue knowing who I am, what I am, and how I fit into His plan for those who need to experience His love and learn more about Him.

After twenty years of fulfilling the call to reach nations, the EITI continues to pursue God's will to touch and transform people and shift old mindsets, presenting the new wineskin. I am grateful that my life has been touched, changed, and activated for God's work and His purposes for me. Each student has their own experiences about how the EITI has impacted them. This journey hasn't just equipped me for ministry—it has revealed the very essence of who I am in Christ. From trembling in the shadows to soaring in purpose, I now walk in the authority of an Eagle who knows her identity, carries her mantle, and lives for God's glory.

Decree and declare these scriptures over your life to experience the joy of discovering who you are.

"Therefore, if anyone is in Christ, he is a new creation. The old has passed away; behold, the new has come" (2 Corinthians 5:17 ESV). I am a new creation because of Jesus Christ, who has made old things disappear. I take hold of the newness of life He has given me to discover and find who I am in Him.

"Therefore, accept each other just as Christ has accepted you, so that God will be given glory" Romans 15:7 NLT. I am accepted, and my identity is in Christ, Jesus. Because of what Jesus did for me, I am convinced that His love will not fail me, nor will the truth of His Word return void regarding who I am in Him.

"For we are God's masterpiece. He has created us anew in Christ Jesus, so we can do the good things he planned for us long ago" (Ephesians 2:10 NLT). I am God's masterpiece, created like a new creation in Jesus. I can do what He has planned for me without problems or doubts. I decree and declare that all doubt and unbelief are gone.

"Nay, in all these things we are more than conquerors through Him that loved us" (Romans 8:37 KJV). I declare that because God loves me, I am more than a conqueror through Jesus Christ.

"For in Christ Jesus you are all sons of God, through faith" (Galatians 3:26 ESV). I declare that I am a son of God, worthy through Jesus Christ and by His glorious grace, adopted into His plan, purpose, and perfect will.

"If your first concern is to look after yourself, you'll never find yourself. But if you forget about yourself and look to me, you'll find both yourself and me" (Matthew 10:39 MSG). Father, I declare that I will look to You first to find who I am, so that I can see You.

ABOUT THE AUTHOR

Jamita Wright founded Adore Him Dance Mobile School. She obtained a BA in English from Virginia State University and an MSA from Central Michigan University. She completed several courses at the Eagles International Training Institute. She has traveled extensively, ministering and prophetically dancing in many nations. Intercession is her life.

www.ingramcontent.com/pod-product-compliance
Lightning Source LLC
Chambersburg PA
CBHW062152080426
42734CB00010B/1655